Acrylic Decorative Painting Techniques

Acrylic Decorative

Painting Techniques

Discover the secrets
of successful
decorative painting

Sybil Edwards

NORTH LIGHT BOOKS
Cincinnati, Ohio

Contents

First published in North America in 1997 by North Light Books, an imprint of F&W Publications, Inc., 1507 Dana Avenue, Cincinnati, OH 452071-800/289-0963

Copyright © 1997 Quarto Inc.

Reprinted 1998
ISBN 0–89134–783–6

This book was designed and produced by
Quarto Publishing plc
The Old Brewery
6 Blundell Street
London N7 9BH

Senior Editor Gerrie Purcell
Senior Art Editor Julie Francis
Designer Roger Daniels
Photographers Paul Forrester, Martin Norris
Illustrators Neil Ballpit, Prue Lester
Picture Research Manager Giulia Hetherington
Editorial Director Mark Dartford
Art Director Moira Clinch

Typeset by Type Technique, London
Manufactured by Regent Publishing Services, Ltd, Hong Kong
Printed by Leefung-Asco Printers Ltd, China

PUBLISHER'S NOTE
The author, copyright holder and publishers have made every effort to ensure that all instructions given in this book are safe and accurate, but they cannot accept legal liability for errors or omissions or for any resulting injury, loss or damage to either property or person whether direct or consequential and howsoever arising. They would like to draw particular attention to the following:

When handling, using or storing paints, mediums, implements or any products mentioned in this book it is strongly advised to always follow the manufacturer's instructions; always store chemicals or similar products securely in their original containers, or clearly marked non-food containers, and keep them well out of reach of children and animals.

When using sprays or aerosol cans ensure eyes and exposed skin are protected. Always work in a well-ventilated area.

Introduction
The Art of Decorative Painting

This tray is a fine example of Rogaland decorative painting, which is a Norwegian-style of Rosemaling.

Decorative painting — in varying styles and using many different techniques — has existed the world over for thousands of years. It has adorned stately homes and grand palaces, holy buildings of many faiths, the abodes of the middle classes, and the humblest of dwellings. Primitive settled groups, and even nomads, used painted decoration to beautify and cheer their surroundings as well as a means of expression.

Nowadays huge numbers of people in many parts of the world enjoy decorative painting as a leisure pursuit. Learning to paint in the different styles that exist from country to country, and even from one locality to another, and discovering the history of various customs and techniques is all part of this fascinating study.

Decorative painting for pleasure first became popular in the United States, and the movement gathered momentum from the 1970s onward, partly by encouraging those who were unsure of their creative skills. Some people move from decorative painting to fine art techniques, but fine artists also find they benefit from the approaches of decorative art. The fact that the two disciplines are coming closer together is expanding the entire repertoire of painted art forms in exciting new directions.

Decorative painting is grounded in the naive styles that are generally known as folk art. But this term has become too narrow for such a varied art form whose styles, techniques, and expressions continue to develop. Just as in fine art we can attribute certain styles to particular artists, the same applies to decorative painting. There are therefore no hard-and-fast

This detail from a design on a large bowl is typical of the Rosemaling style of decoration.

formulas for the production of this art, but learning methods do tend to follow an established procedure which derives from the folk art tradition. At the heart of that tradition lies strokework, and this is still regarded as the best starting point for the decorative painter.

For many artists, disciplined strokework is the alpha and omega of painting, and the gentle, rhythmic movement is an addictive therapy in itself. Certainly there is much to perfect and enjoy in this defined area. The Rosemaling styles of Scandinavia, for example, entail a dedicated commitment to strokework — just as a pianist might specialize in the work of Mozart rather than performing across the wider musical repertoire.

Current advances in decorative art have been made possible by new paints and products, but also by imagination. And once you are competent at strokework, you can move on into the more nebulous zone of stroke suggestion, and beyond.

The purpose of this book is to familiarize you with the choices that decorative art has to offer. The techniques are fully illustrated, so that they are easy to follow and to learn. You may eventually decide to focus on traditional folk art painting, but you are just as likely to develop your

own decorative art style by integrating techniques no one had thought of trying before!

The techniques are divided into three main sections: strokes; bold painting; and blending strokes. Strokework is our first port of call for traditional reasons as well as its importance to good painting practice. The limitation of strokework is in the expression of images. Beyond florals, foliage, and ornaments, and without the addition of blending techniques, it remains a two-dimensional style. Its strength is its impressionistic and design capabilities, so if these are the aspects that appeal to you, you will enjoy this part of the book.

If you prefer a wide array of images, including people and objects, you can use the bold painting section as your initial starting point. Strokework can be used with these techniques, but it is easy to refer back to the strokes as you need them. The techniques of bold painting are simple to learn. The subjects are extremely varied, and often amusing, and enable you to introduce the rudiments of form.

The blending section shows you how to emphasize form and give your work a three-dimensional appearance. Some painters choose to go straight

Another beautiful example of good strokework and choice of color scheme.

from strokework to blending, so intent are they on achieving a realistic, or *trompe l'oeil,* look.

If you learn the techniques from all three sections you will become a fully-fledged decorative artist; if you learn techniques from one or two sections, you will be able to while away many happy hours; and some of you, we hope, will make these pages the basis for your own experiments and adventures in decorative art.

Decorative painting is an enjoyable form of painting. Many of the attractive examples in this book, such as this trinket box (see p. 58) will inspire you. But, whether you want to study this art form as a hobby or more seriously — practice of the strokes and blending techniques is the key to success.

Before You Start

Decorative painting is a leisure pursuit but in our bustling world, leisure is often intermittent and short-lived. Most people cannot spare a lot of setting up and cleaning time, or a dedicated work space in their houses. Manufacturers have borne these factors in mind in developing products that reflect a busy lifestyle. They have developed easy-to-clean paints and useful time-saving equipment, such as stay-wet palettes. Refer to the basic equipment list on pages 10–11, and you will find you can begin decorative painting in a small way without upsetting the household, and your first forays need not be expensive. There is time enough to invest in specialized items if you decide to become a serious decorative artist. You will need to allow time and space to ensure a positive experience and to develop your confidence, but you will gradually appreciate the ease with which you can fit painting into your everyday life.

Equipment

To help you decide if you are going to enjoy decorative art, experiment with some strokework before you spend money on supplies. Practice some of the strokes and motifs on pp. 52–93. The items you will need for a trial run and the equipment for additional work are shown here and over.

Basic supplies

1 Background paints *Painting background colors, especially on large objects, naturally uses up more paint than painting decoratively. Some manufacturers produce a range of background paints in pots big enough to dip a large basing brush. For color conversion between the main brand names, please see pp. 18–19.*

2 Brushes *Even your first trials should be carried out with a good-quality brush in order to avoid disappointment. Synthetic brushes designed for use with acrylic paints are reasonably priced. Their chemical structure is more suitable for acrylics than natural hairs are, and they are less prone to breakage.*

The main brush brands include brushes specifically for decorative art, but their sizes vary, which can be bewildering for a beginner. What you want is a standard-size round brush, flat brush, and liner. A good stockist should be able to advise.

3 Paper *Any type of art paper or even clean scraps, just for practicing.*

4 Clean jar *To fill with water for rinsing brushes, preferably one that is not too tall.*

5 Basic palette knife *An implement for mixing paint, such as a knife or lollipop stick.*

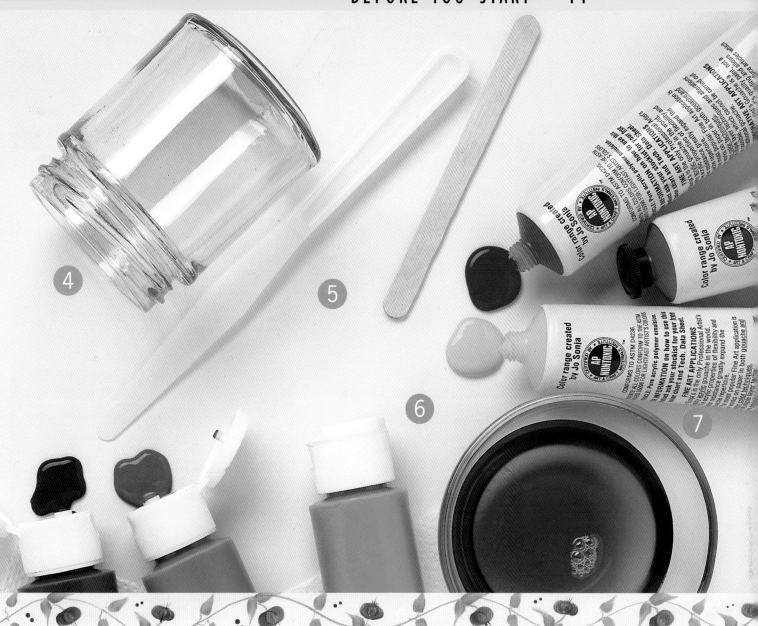

6 Acrylic paints *Especially brands developed specifically for decorative painting, are recommended. They are easy to work with, have good coverability, dry to a matte finish in comfortable painting time, and most are of an artist's quality. They are easy to clean up, and most important, can be used on a variety of surfaces. Your choice will be limited if your stockist carries only one brand. Even if there is a variety of brands you will then need to choose the format; pack, tube or bottle. For color conversion between the main brand names, please see pp. 18–19.*

Water-based acrylic paints are especially suitable for decorative art and much easier to use than oils. You can dispense a choice of colors onto a stay-wet palette (see p. 13) that will remain usable for two or three days. The brushes clean readily in cold water with mild soap. If you only have an hour to spare, these are the time-saving factors that count. And with water-based paints, you can set yourself up at the kitchen table if necessary.

7 Clean-up equipment *Paper towels (kitchen paper) for blotting excess water out of brushes. Mild soap for cleaning brushes, especially when acrylic-based paints are used.*

Simple paint palette *A shallow surface on which to dispense the paint, such as an old plate or a plastic meat tray from the supermarket.*

Simple blending palette *A flat, smooth surface on which to blend paint into the brush.*

Additional equipment

* Entries with an asterisk are items which will upgrade your basic supplies if you want to take your painting more seriously.

1 A pattern *Either your own design or one from the thousands of pattern packs available, which cover just about any subject and style you can think of. The packs include the pattern, a full-color photograph of the finished object, a list of materials, and complete instructions, often accompanied by step-by-step illustrations. Also you can refer to pp. 120–25 for some of the patterns used in this book.*

2* Permanent pen or brush pen *Used for fine outlining. The pen is usually fiber-tipped. Brush pens are loaded with a cartridge for a constant flow of color.*

3 Tracing paper *For copying patterns and transferring them onto the prepared surface you want to paint.*

4* Graphite paper *Think of carbon paper! It's different in that the surface is a fine chalk residue which will erase. Never use carbon paper.*

5 Soft pencil *Usually a 2B or 4B is fine to make a tracing of a pattern.*

6 Brown paper bag for sanding *This is to rub down your painted background to ensure a smooth surface for your painted design. Even the finest sand paper would be too rough.*

7 Colored chalk pencil *For outlining a design directly onto the surface to be painted and also to back a traced design with chalk, so that when you retrace over the design the chalk will transfer onto the surface.*

8 Eraser *To erase the pencil or chalk marks which may still show after your painting has dried.*

9* Extender medium *A chemical solution used to extend the drying time of acrylic paints. (See p. 14 for more information on mediums.)*

10* Varnish *To protect the finished item. See pp. 30–31 for more details.*

11 All-purpose sealer *This liquid is used to seal the blank (see pp. 22–23) before applying either acrylic- or water-based paint.*

12* Bubble palette *A palette with at least two dish indents for clean water and extender, or for additional substances needed in small quantities.*

13* Additional brushes *As your interest develops, you will want to add specialized brushes to your collection (see p. 32.)*

14* Brush tub (basin) *This has a bowl for water to clean your brushes and slots to hold them to dry.*

15* Hairdryer *To reduce the drying time of paints – and especially useful when doing a cracklure (craquelure) varnish (see p. 39).*

16* Waxed paper palette booklet *To use for blending. This will replace your blending palette. The waxed sheets are disposable.*

17 Blanks *A fresh surface to paint is known as a blank, and there are thousands of examples available from craft stores or through craft magazines and directories. Blanks can be made of wood or particleboard, also called medium density fiberboard (MDF). The variety of blanks is enormous, ranging from bottle racks to desks, tables and screens. Don't be too ambitious your first few times – keep to small items until your expertise builds.*

You may be tempted to paint an old item. If it is covered with varnish or paint, you will need to determine what the underneath surface is and whether it is compatible with the paint you are using. For the inexperienced, it is best to begin with virgin wood or blanks.

18* Trowel-style palette knife *To enable the easy mixture of paints.*

19* Stylus *A very fine-tipped implement for making pinprick dots.*

20* Stay-wet palette *From art supply stores, in place of your improvised paint palette. This allows you to continue using the same paints for several days.*

21* Cleaning spirit *For getting rid of mistakes or refurbishing neglected brushes, you need a spirit such as rubbing alcohol (surgical spirit) or denatured alcohol (methylated spirits.)*

22 Masking tape *To fix the trace pattern securely onto your surface. Do not press down too firmly, when masking tape is lifted off it should not have damaged your background.*

Mediums

As you become better acquainted with various techniques and styles of painting, you will discover the value of working with mediums. These are substances that are added to acrylic paints to make them more versatile and adapt them to the job on hand. They can smooth, protect, alter the surface texture, or extend drying time. There is a wide variety to choose from, and most of the paint manufacturers produce them. Be sure to read the manufacturer's instructions before use.

Flow medium

Flow medium is used in place of water for a smoothing effect. You may have noticed with normal stroke procedure that brushmarks occur along with the strokes. This is quite an attractive feature, but sometimes you might want a more even appearance. To achieve it, dampen your brush with flow medium instead of water before loading with paint. Flow medium is also helpful for the production of long, flowing, unbroken brushwork.

Clear glazing medium

This medium has a number of uses. For the beginner, it serves as a handy protection device. For example, if you are worried about spoiling a part of the design that you have already applied when you still have more to do, an application of clear glazing medium offers some protection. You can go on painting, removing any mistakes, without damaging the work underneath.

Clear glazing medium is also utilized for transparent glazing and woodstain effects. Mix it with pigment to produce a light film of color that allows the background to show through. If you are working on an attractively grained piece of wood, this can be most rewarding.

Textile medium

This allows you to paint on fabric of acrylic/cotton blends.

Glass and tile painting medium

This enables you to paint on glass and ceramics. It is mixed with the pigments to create a permanent surface.

Extender medium (or retarder and antiquing medium)

This dual-purpose medium is extremely helpful. Used as a retarder, it delays the drying time of the pigment with which it is mixed. This is invaluable for blending work, or creating smooth effects.

Taking advantage of the extended drying time, it can also be mixed with pigments such as burnt umber and applied to produce an antiqued finish.

RIGHT and CENTER: These wonderful floral designs are details from decorative work done on tin.

ABOVE: Most of the major manufacturers produce a full range of mediums. The range above includes, from left to right, flow, antiquing, glass, textile and clear glazing.

LEFT: This detail of work on an apron shows a fine example of painting on fabric using a textile medium.

Color Theory

Those whose chief pleasure in life is messing about with paints are likely to take any detour to reach the mixing vat and tend to get so sidetracked that they wonder where the time went. Pigments and colors are recognized for their distinctive behavior, which is surprisingly wide-ranging, and the sensitive artist can form a unique relationship with them.

Entire books are written on color theory, but here we will introduce you to a few of the basic principles, so that you can begin work with a limited expenditure on paints. You will soon realize that the limited palette is like planting a seed: from three kernels of paint alone – red, blue and yellow – a whole world of color magic explodes.

Plus White

The colors to buy

The colors shown in the painted examples in this book need not be copied — work with the colors which are a close match or experiment with your own color schemes.

You do not need to spend a lot of money on acrylic paints to start decorative painting. Five basic pigments are all you need to mix a vast palette of colors. They are: red, blue, yellow, black and white.

You will find that there are many reds, blues and yellows to select from. You should look for a "true" version of each, and if you are uncertain, match the colors as closely as you can to the color wheel on the opposite page. Look at the wheel as a clockface — the "true" primary colors are at the following clock positions: yellow is at 11 to 1 o'clock; blue is at 4 to 5 o'clock; and red is at 7 to 8 o'clock.

Black and white

Technically speaking, black and white are not colors, but nevertheless we treat them as if they were. We include them in the basic palette because they are useful as a quick means of toning up or toning down color. Quick methods, however, are not always ideal solutions. As you learn more about color theory, more subtle and fascinating options will become apparent.

Simple color theory

Most decorative painters start out with the intention to learn color theory and mix their own colors. In truth, however, they are usually so keen to get on with painting that they take every practical shortcut – and avoiding the color-mixing process is number one on the hit list.

The major brands have enormous color ranges and they take care not to replicate one another too closely by producing tones and shades which vary slightly. This means that you can usually find the color you need.

Although manufacturers recommend that you do not mix brands, on the whole, most acrylics seem to be compatible.

When you buy a pattern pack, you can open it up, refer to the "materials needed" section, and buy the recommended colors straight off the shelf in one operation. Then you can go home and set to work

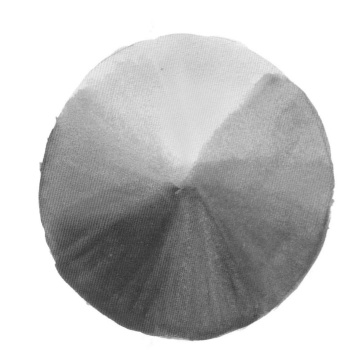

Primary colors

It is suggested that you buy red, blue and yellow because these are primary colors. Primary colors are to painting what elements are to chemistry. They cannot be broken down into component parts, but from these three basics the entire color universe is built.

The basic color wheel

*The color wheel shows how all of the colors derive from the three basic **primary colors**; red, blue, and yellow. The **secondary colors** are made by mixing two primaries, half and half.*

Tertiary colors are mixed using two secondaries, half and half (see the swatches below the color wheel.)

without the bothersome preliminary of mixing paint. It also means that the right color is on hand for every painting session until completion of the project. If you mix your own colors, there may be some variation between sessions.

After a time, you may find that color increasingly draws your attention, and you begin to tune into its mysterious nature. This is evidence that there is no prescribed order for learning, merely that we should be open when interest beckons. At such a time, you can return to this section and read about color theory for the serious painter.

The secondary and tertiary examples are merely halfway stages. There are many degrees between them which we have omitted.

Looking at the secondary colors, you will see that the colors are less intense. Green has appeared, so that now you can paint stems and leaves to primary-colored flowers in red, blue, and yellow.

The tertiary colors are even less vivid. These are known as earth colors, generally more suitable for backgrounds than the primaries or secondaries. If you mixed the tertiaries half and half, the colors would grow more somber still, and would eventually become dark gray. Surprisingly, mixing all of the primaries together in equal proportions achieves the same result – those beautiful lively colors turn to sludge! This is just one of the many discoveries that you can make by experimenting with color.

It takes quite a lot of mixing to create earth colors and their darker blends. If these are the colors you like for backgrounds, and especially if your item is large, it makes more sense to buy them ready-mixed, or you will use up your primary colors too quickly. For small quantities, on the other hand, mixing your own from an established palette can take less time.

Acrylic Color Conversion Chart

JO SONJA'S CHROMA ACRYLICS	LIQUITEX	DECOART AMERICANO	DELTA CERAMCOAT	CHROMA PAINTS
Amethyst	Medium Magenta + Brilliant Purple (1:1)	Orchid	Lilac Dust	128 Maroon
Aqua	Turquoise	Desert Turquoise	Laguna	144 Sea Green
Brilliant Green	Christmas Green	Holly Green	Jubilee Green	153 Perm Green Light
Brown Earth	Burnt Umber	Dark Chocolate	Brown Iron Oxide	167 Burnt Sienna
Burgundy	Deep Brilliant Red	Cranberry Wine	Sweetheart Blush	123 Deep Brilliant Red
Burnt Sienna	Burnt Sienna	Burnt Sienna	Burnt Sienna	167 Burnt Sienna
Burnt Umber	Burnt Umber	Burnt Umber	Walnut	161 Burnt Umber
Cad Scarlet	Scarlet Red + Napthol Red Light (5:1)	Cadmium Red	Blaze	115 Scarlet
Yellow Light	Yellow Light Hansa	Lemon Yellow	Bright Yellow	102 Lemon Yellow
Cad Yellow Mid	Brilliant Yellow	Cadmium Yellow	Yellow	105 Cadmium Yellow Medium
Carbon Black	Mars Black	Ebony	Black	176 Chroma Black
Cobalt Blue	Brilliant Blue Purple	True Blue	Pthalo Blue	137 Cobalt Blue
Colony Blue	Brilliant Blue + Burnt Umber (2:1)	Desert Turquoise	Avalon	142 Turquoise Blue
Dioxazine Purple	Dioxazine Purple	Dioxazine Purple	Purple	132 Dioxazine Purple
French Blue	Payne's Gray + Manganese Blue Hue + Ultramarine (2:2:1)	Navy Blue + Crim Tide	Nightfall	140 Manganese Blue
Gold Oxide	Raw Sienna + Scarlet + Unbleached Titanium (3:1:1)	Terracotta	Mexicana	165 Venetian Red
Green Oxide	Chromium Oxide Green	Mistletoe	Chrome Green Light	150 Chromium Green Oxide
Indian Red Oxide	Burgundy + Burnt Umber (1:1)	Rookwood	Candy Bar	166 Red Iron Oxide
Jade	Bright Aqua Green + Chromium Green Oxide (3:1)	Jade + Wedgewood Blue	Leprechaun	158 Olive Green Light
Napthol Crimson	Napthol Crimson	Napthol Red	Tompte Red	120 Napthol Crimson
Napthol Red Light	Scarlket + Napthol Red Light (4:1)	Berry Red	Napthol Crimson	116 Cadmium Red Medium
Nimbus Gray	Unbleached Titanium + Manganese Blue Hue (1:1)	Slate Gray + Mink Tan	Lichen Gray	171 Warm Gray
Norwegian Orange	Red Oxide + Scarlet (1:1)	Burnt Orange + Calico	GA Clay + NAP RD LT	119 Chroma Red Deep

A secondary color and the one primary color which is not used to make the color are known as **complementary colors**. Adding small amounts of secondary color to its opposite primary tones it down.

Adding black to a color also tones it down, although strictly speaking, we should say it changes the color's value, or produces a shade of that color. In the same way, adding white to a color lightens its value, or produces a tint. Mixing black and white together in various proportions results in a range of gray values. Adding a gray value to a color produces a tone of that color.

If this basic explanation of color theory has whetted your appetite, go to your library and delve more deeply into this fascinating subject. But be careful to select a book about color as it relates to pigments or paints, and not to light or photography, where the rules are different.

Toning color up or down

Look at the primaries in the color wheel again and take note of the secondary colors: green, violet and orange.

JO SONJA'S CHROMA ACRYLICS	LIQUITEX	DECOART AMERICANO	DELTA CERAMCOAT	CHROMA PAINTS
Payne's Gray	Payne's Gray	Uniform Blue	Midnight	173 Payne's Gray
Pine Green	Yellow Light Hansa + Manganese Blue Hue (5:1)	Avocado	Dark Jungle	147 Hooker's Green
Plum Pink	Viridian + Manganese Blue Hue (2:1)	Raspberry	Dusty Mauve	127 Magenta Deep
Provincial Beige		Sable Brown	Territorial Beige	162 Vandyke Brown
Prussian Blue	Ultramarine Blue + Burnt Umber (2:1)	Navy Blue	Prussian Blue	134 Prussian Blue
Pthalo Blue	Pthalo Cyanine Blue	True Blue	Manganese Blue	135 Pthalo Blue
Pthalo Green	Pthalo Cyanine Green	Viridian Green	Pthalo Green	145 Pthalo Green
Raw Sienna	Brilliant Yellow + Burnt Sienna (4:1)	T Cotta + Dark Choc	Raw Sienna	160 Raw Sienna
Raw Umber	Raw Umber	Dark Chocolate	Dark Chocolate	164 Raw Umber
Red Earth	Red Oxide	Brandywine	Red Iron Oxide	166 Red Iron Oxide
Rich Gold		Venetian Gold/M	Gold/M	
Sapphire		Victorian Blue	Liberty Blue	134 Prussian Blue
Silver	Silver Met	Shimmering Silver/M	Silver/M	
Smoked Pearl		Antique White	Sandstone	178 Parchment
Titanium White	Titanium White	Snow White	White	179 Titanium White
Trans Magenta	Raspberry	Sizz Pink + Vic Blue	USA PK + SWHT Blush	124 Rose
Turner's Yellow	Turner's Yellow	Antique Gold + Cad Yellow	Empire Gold	109 Gamboge New
Ultra Blue Deep	Ultramarine Blue	Ultra Blue Deep	Ultra Blue	136 Ultramarine
Ultramarine	Brilliant Blue Purple	True Blue	Ultra Blue	136 Ultramarine
Vermilion	Scarlet + Brilliant Yellow (3:1)	Cad Orange + Tangerine	Tangerine	117 Vermilion
Warm White	Soft White	Buttermilk	Antique White	178 Parchment
Yellow Light	Brilliant Yellow	Lemon Yellow	Bright Yellow	103 Cadmium Yellow Light
Yellow Oxide	Yellow Oxide	Antique Gold	Antique Gold	159 Yellow Ochre

Preparation and Backgrounds

You have designed or selected a pattern you want to paint.
You have chosen a color scheme. And you have found a blank
(see p. 12) to paint it onto. This will probably be made of
wood or particleboard (MDF). (The instructions given here
are for these surfaces, so if you are using metal or ceramics,
refer to the product labels for any slight differences in
preparation.) Although you are probably eager to start
painting, you must prepare the blank first. Luckily, this does
not take long, since the products involved are designed to
make the process as easy as possible.
Always remember that good preparation makes for better end
results, so practicing the following techniques will pay
dividends later.

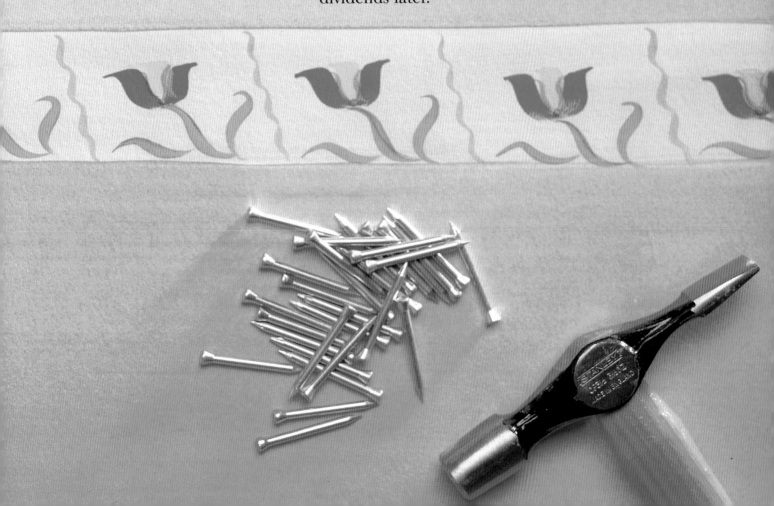

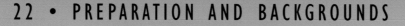

Preparation Procedure

Preparation makes a bit of a mess, so protect your work surfaces with newspaper. After you finish, be sure to clean up thoroughly, or when you come to paint, stray fragments may find their way onto your work.

Materials: *wood filler, fine-grade sandpaper, water-based wood sealer or all-purpose sealer, acrylic- or water-based paint, 2in (5cm) brush for background painting or 2in (5cm) foam brush, brown paper bag, damp cloth.*

You might want to impart an older look to your object by distressing it first, which will take a little more time. Alternatively, you can antique it after decoration (see pp. 38–39). Distressing can be done in a number of ways. Bang the object here and there with a hammer, leaving a few dents. Take a large nail, and hammer some nail holes. Purposely choose a rough blank and do not sand it. Do not fill in any holes. Distressing can be a studious art form, just like the teenager's blue jeans, holed, torn, and gashed in all the right places!

1 **If you want a smooth, unblemished finished piece then the surface must be perfectly smooth from the start. First, fill any unsightly holes with wood filler.**

2 **Sand when dry with a brown paper bag or fine-grade sandpaper, following the grain of the wood. If your object has the look or feel of peach fuzz, do not try and sand it off at this stage – it will only encourage more growth.**

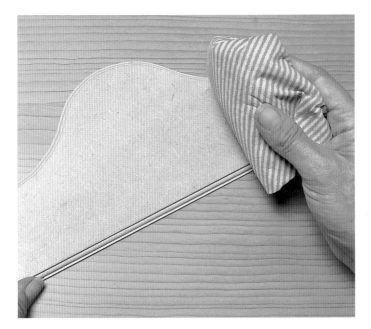

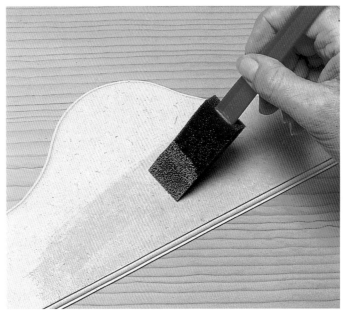

3 Wipe the object very lightly with damp lint-free cloth to remove any sanding dust. Particleboard (MDF) is particularly prone to retaining a fine film of dust. Be thorough but gentle.

4 Seal the wood with a water-based wood sealer. Use a foam brush to impart a smooth surface, or a conventional brush if you prefer a hint of brushmarks. Because the sealer is a water-based product, it sets fairly quickly, so work purposefully, and avoid going over areas that are partially dry. You will know when drying has begun because the wet sealer begins to lose its sheen.

When the sealer is dry, sand the areas that had peach fuzz with the bag. Stiffened now with dry sealer, the fuzz can be removed without drawing out the wood fiber underneath. Always sand gently with the wood grain. Remove dust with a damp cloth. Apply a second coat of sealer if necessary.

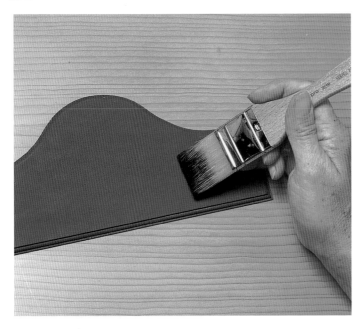

5 Apply three thin, colored basecoats. Allow each coat to dry between applications, and sand it with a brown paper bag. Use a hairdryer to speed drying, but let the object return to room temperature before painting the next coat. To encourage smooth application, dip your brush in water, blot out the excess, then lower it into the paint just over halfway up the hairs. Apply until the paint stops spreading easily, then dip, reload, and paint again. As with the sealer, the paint is quick-drying, so work positively. Unless you want to impart a faux finish background (see pp. 34–37), your object is now ready for the pattern.

Before You Paint

Here is a simple guide for you to follow when setting up your work station and paint palette. When you have gained experience you can adapt them to your own method of working. A store-bought stay-wet palette is a good investment, but why not try to make your own first (see opposite).

Preparing a paint palette

1 Dispense the colors for your project onto your paint palette. You only need a small amount of each, well spaced out on the palette.

2 Prepare any color mixtures on your mixing palette. Squeeze a small amount of the main color onto the palette. Then add a tiny amount of the secondary color(s). Mix thoroughly with a palette knife.

Preparing your work station

Fill a jar with water for cleaning your brushes, and position it to your right if you are right-handed. Use a squat jar rather than a tall one – there is less chance of accidentally knocking it over.

Pour some water into a bottle cap and place it close to your work. This is to freshen your brush and keep it damp as you paint. The cleaning jar soon gets dirty and water from that could muddy your colors.

Position the blending palette to your right if you are right-handed.

Fold a square of paper towel in quarters, and keep it near or tucked under your blending palette. This will serve as a blotter for excess water in the brush.

3 Use the flat side of the knife, and smash the paint on the palette. This is not as brutal as it sounds. As you smash, the paint spreads over the palette. Then use the sharp side of the knife to marshal the partially mixed paint back into a pile, and repeat the smashing.

4 Eventually the paint will be mixed to your satisfaction. Scoop it up and put it onto your paint palette.

How to make a stay-wet palette

You can make your own stay-wet palette. Take a shallow plastic container with a lid, and cut a thin household sponge to the same shape. Dampen the sponge and put it at the bottom of the container. Place a piece of damp cardboard or paper of equal size on top of the sponge. Dispense your paint onto the cardboard. Replace the lid when you finish painting. This palette is now set up for 2–3 days. In very hot climates, keep it in the refrigerator between painting sessions.

Pattern Application

Patterns provide a design for you to follow. They also help you to position your work correctly on the surface you are planning to paint.

1 Transfer the pattern onto tracing paper, and position the tracing paper on your object. This enables you to match up lines already traced onto the object through the tracing paper, if you need to reposition the pattern.

2 Fix the pattern into position with masking tape in two or three places.

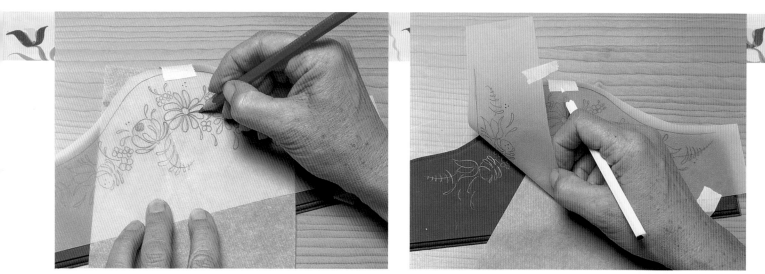

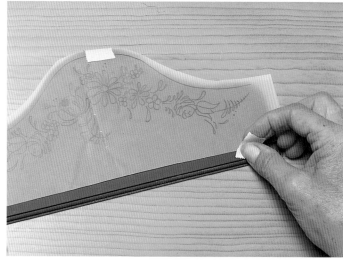

3 Insert a sheet of graphite paper between the pattern and the object — chalky side down. Alternatively, before attaching the pattern, chalk over the back of the pattern lines with a chalk pencil. Use the pencil at a slant when going over the outline on the tracing paper or pattern sheet to expose as much chalk outline on the object's surface as possible.

4 Trace on the lines of the main image only with a soft pencil. Avoid pressing too hard – you do not want to dent your object with pencil marks. A colored chalk pencil will help you to see the lines that you have already traced (it is amazing how you can forget). Remove the pattern and the graphite paper. Now comes the excitement. It is time to start painting.

Painting a decoration

With practice, you will soon realize that the ratio of paint to water in your brush determines how easy it is to complete a stroke. It varies according to surface. Porous surfaces need more water; smooth ones less.

 **1** Select your brush and dip it in water. Always wet the brush before putting it into paint. This prevents the paint from gumming up the hairs at the top near the metal ferrule, and thus lengthens the life of your brushes. Blot out the excess water on the paper towel.

2 Check that no droplets have adhered to the ferrule, and if so wipe them off. They have a habit of running into your brush just as you are making the perfect stroke and turning it into a watery mess.

3 Pick up a small amount of paint from the paint palette.

4 Blend the paint into the brush on the palette by stroking it back and forth to tease the paint into the hairs. You may need to repeat this exercise two or three times to load up enough paint. As you blend, draw the hairs into a point. Avoid overloading the brush. It will look bloated, and your stroke will not tail off cleanly.

5 Try painting a comma stroke (see pp. 54-55). The brush flattens first as you apply pressure, then returns to a point as the pressure is released. But the point will probably be fractionally blunter than it was at the start.

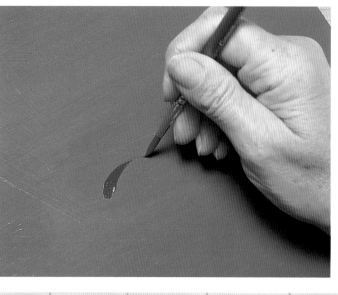

6 Reblend on the paint palette over the same spot of wet paint. This evenly redistributes the paint already in the brush and reshapes the hairs into a pristine point. Paint another stroke. You will be able to paint several strokes before you need to pick up more paint, but reblend between each stroke to keep paint and brush in prime condition. It is sometimes possible to get away without reblending, but judging when will only come with experience. Paint a border to test out the procedure.

7 Clean your brush in the jar. Washing out your brush is only necessary when you are going to use a new color, or if you get too much paint in the brush and need to start again, or if you have been painting with the same color for some time and it begins to congeal or go grainy. You will be able to judge this with experience.

You can be fairly vigorous, but avoid action that might damage the hairs, such as scrubbing them around on the bottom of the jar. You can use the jar base to help you, but tease gently in the direction of the hairs as you nudge them against the jar to dislodge the paint.

8 Blot out any dirty water left on the brush onto a piece of paper towel.

9 Dip the brush into your clean water source. Blot out the excess. In some atmospheric conditions, you may need a tiny drop more water for reblending.

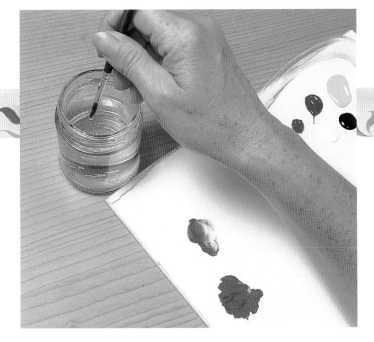

10 Touch only the very tip of the brush in the clean water. The minutest amount will be enough to facilitate the blending of the paint already in the hairs.

11 If you pick up too much water, blot it out, pick up a bit more paint if necessary, and then reblend. When the decoration is complete, you can protect your work with varnish, as described on the following pages. If you want to apply an antique or speckled finish first, turn to pp. 38–39.

Varnishing

Varnishing is not essential. You may prefer a less finished look. But varnishing does protect and can enhance your work. You can choose a matte, satin, or gloss finish, and add a final patina of wax if you wish.

Here, we explain two methods of varnishing: one using an acrylic spray varnish, and the other a water-based varnish which is brushed on. The choice of sheen is largely a matter of personal preference. Satin is the safe option, providing sufficient sheen to enhance the decoration but not so much that it glares. Matte is a good choice if you want to protect your work and go on to apply a waxed finish.

Preparation for varnishing

1 **Erase all of the pattern lines.** Some can be wiped away with a dampened soft cloth or paper towel. Others are more stubborn. The lines of graphite paper, for example, may need encouragement from a kneaded eraser (putty eraser), soap and water, or a mineral spirit (white spirit).

METHOD • I

Acrylic Spray

The advantage of spray varnish is that you can apply it fairly soon after completing the decoration without risk of smudging. A word of caution, however: acrylic paint that has not dried for a full 24 hours might affect the varnish over time. Always read the manufacturer's label before use.

The advantages of sprays are obvious: there is no measuring, and little mess or cleaning up. Protect the surrounding area with newspaper. Work in a well-ventilated area – or better still, outdoors on a dry day. You should also wear a protective mask.

The spray dries so quickly that you can apply a second coat almost as soon as you finish the first, so plan your spraying to avoid newspaper drying onto your work.

1 The spray can must be held upright, so position your piece accordingly. You may need to arrange a system of props. Spray back and forth across the object in even swathes, taking care to avoid varnish building up anywhere. It is better to move along steadily and catch any missed areas with successive applications. A number of thin coats is more successful than one or two thick ones.

2 Remove any dirt or dust. Do not apply finishes in a dusty atmosphere, because particles can adhere to the wet varnish. Lay down some newspaper to protect your work area.

METHOD • 2

Acrylic Varnish

Water-based acrylic varnishes dry much more quickly than their oil-based counterparts. The coats of varnish brush on more thickly than spray varnishes, enabling a good buildup as well as being cost effective.

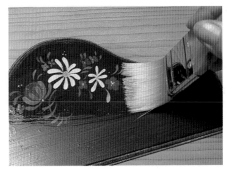

1 *Allow the decorated piece to dry for 24 hours. Stir the varnish in the container. This is better than shaking, because it minimizes air bubbles. Pour the amount required into a jar or jar lid. Use a large painter's brush whose hairs will not drop out. Dip it in water and blot out the excess. Dip the brush into the varnish halfway up the hairs.*

2 *Apply the varnish in sections, smoothing over each area in a slip-slap motion. Apply the second coat when the first is dry – after about 10–15 minutes. Allow a little more time before the third coat.*

To be safe, check the manufacturer's instructions.

Care of Materials and Brushes

All good painters know that if you look after your equipment and paints, all you need to concentrate on is technique, strokework and enjoying your painting. But, if you are sloppy about cleaning up after each painting session, the paint hardens and you will have a difficult job. Not much fun!

Round brush

Short liner

Lettering

Long liner

Spotter

Brush care

Brushes are the most important tools of decorative painting. If they are to work for you at optimum efficiency and last as long as they should, you need to observe a few basic principles.

Clean your brushes thoroughly after every painting session, or paint will build up at the point where the ferrule (see p. 43) and hairs meet like plaque at the base of a tooth. You cannot just swish them through water, and expect them to remain effective.

Decorative painters are often a sociable group who go on painting bees, getting together to work. If you plan to travel around with your brushes, it is worth acquiring a brush travel case to ensure that your essential tools stay in good condition.

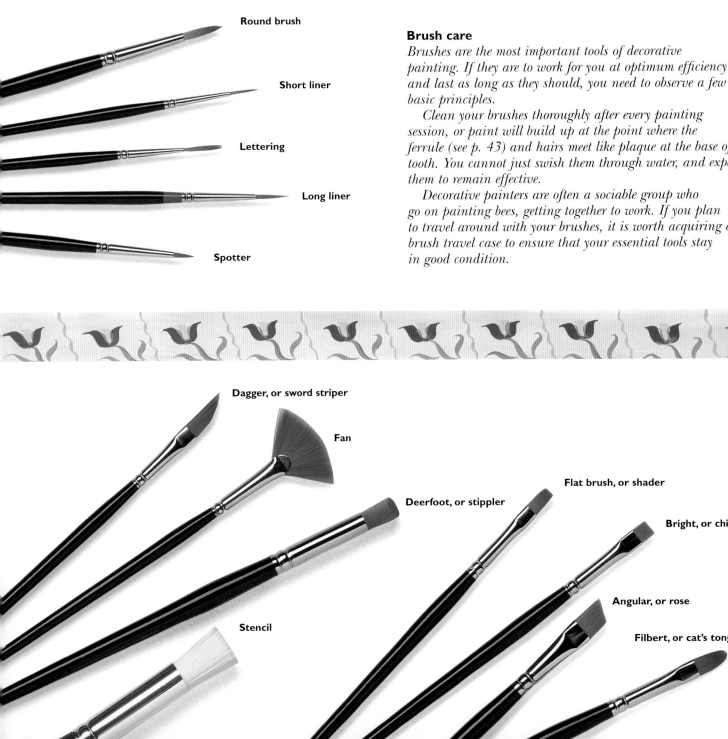

Dagger, or sword striper

Fan

Deerfoot, or stippler

Flat brush, or shader

Bright, or chisel

Angular, or rose

Filbert, or cat's tongue

Stencil

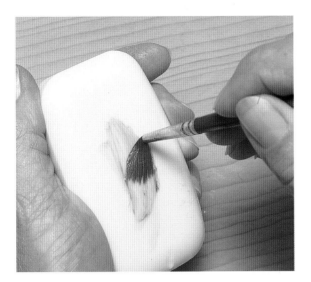

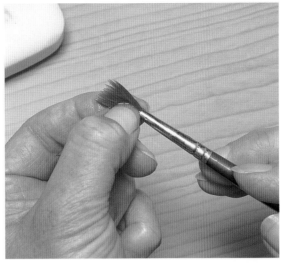

2 Your thumb-nail can help to comb through the hairs. Rinse the hairs well. Repeat if necessary until you can no longer see any hint of discoloration in the soap.

1 Run clean cold water over the brushes. Do not use hot water, because this "cooks" the paint onto the hairs. It may also damage the glue which holds them inside the ferrule. Rinsing removes most of the paint, but a residue will accumulate over time without proper care.

Complete the job with a bar of mild soap. Stroke the soap gently into the hairs using your fingers to massage it into the area where paint particles collect. Be gentle, and work in the direction of the hairs.

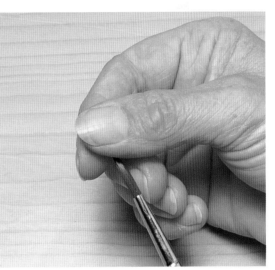

3 When the brush is clean, smooth it into its original shape. You can use a little soap. Store the brush upright in a jar. Rinse out the soap at the start of the next painting session.

Water receptacles

Pour out the water and wash the containers. The jar used for cleaning brushes will be very messy, with paint particles having settled and adhered to the underwater surfaces.

Out of concern for the environment, and to guard against drain blockages, it is a good idea to reserve a large tub for use as a dirty water dump bin. Filter out the water when the bin is full, and dispose of the paint residue safely.

Blending palette

If you used a waxed paper palette, tear the sheet off and dispose of it. If your blending palette is a reusable one, soak it in water. After a short time, most of the paint will bubble and lift off. Some pigments are more stubborn and will need scrubbing with soap.

Paint palette

If you have a reusable paint palette, soak it and scrub off stubborn paint using a little soap. Thoroughly rinse it.

If you are using a stay-wet palette, dispose of the sheet holding the colors. Thoroughly rinse the sponge. Store your stay-wet palette with the lid off.

Backgrounds

Today's decorative painting is a versatile art, and its repertoire includes a range of background effects. Although plain backgrounds are still popular, they can be replaced with an assortment of exciting choices to complement your decoration.

You can imitate material such as marble or wood grain – a faux (or false) effect – or create a design from your own imagination. Structural paints make embossing an easy task. Stamp products are available for introducing pretty repeat patterns. Pen brushes, fitted with a cartridge, are a revolutionary new product if you want to short-circuit the sometimes tedious repetition of loading your brush, especially when working with one color over a relatively large area.

The major manufacturers cater specifically to the decorative painter's need for a good range of colors for either plain or special-effect backgrounds. These paints are available in conveniently sized pots with an opening suitable for a large brush. Gone are the days of mixing background colors from several tubes with the wastage that occurred because you did not use it all.

The background effects illustrated here are only a few of the possibilities, but will give you some ideas for your own experiments.

Stippling

A stippled effect is applied over a background color. Ideally, you will use a stippling brush, which has stiff bristles shaved flat. An alternative is an old brush whose hairs shoot out in all directions like rampant weed. Chop the hairs off flat with a razor knife.

1 Choose your colors: a light background with darker stipples, or a dark background with lighter stipples. Apply three coats of background color.

2 Touch the end of the brush hairs to the paint, taking care not to pick up too much paint. Tap the brush up and down over a practice sheet of paper to release a scatter of speckles. They should appear even and clean. If there is too much paint in the brush, the hairs stick together, producing a globby rather than a crisp effect. Once the specks are satisfactory, begin on your piece. Tap in strips, being careful not to bend the bristles, which would create smudges.

Sponging

A sponged effect can be produced by two methods, or both combined, as in this example: sponging off and sponging on.

1 Choose contrasting colors, for example, yellow and green. Paint on three coats of background. Once dry, apply your chosen contrasting color, mixed with a little retarder to delay the drying time.

2 Dampen a sea sponge, squeezing out the excess water, and use it to blot off the paint just applied. Twist your wrist as you work to achieve a more random effect. This is sponging off.

3 Dry this with a hairdryer. Now we add the sponged on effect. Use a brush to transfer some more of the color just used onto your sponge. Lightly touch some of this paint onto the sponged off surface in random applications.

Random rag drops

This is a subtle effect created on a washed background (see pp. 100–101).

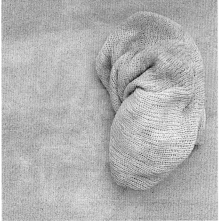

1 Apply one or two coats of color wash. Use a water spray to keep the surface damp.

2 Drop a cotton dishcloth randomly onto the surface to create faint, washed-out effects here and there.

3 Once you are happy with the mottled background allow to dry. Remember not to be too fussy and continue – the effect should be random and subtle.

Combing

The combed effect can be created as a series of wavy lines, or you can use your thumbnail or another implement to produce a design in the upper layer of wet paint.

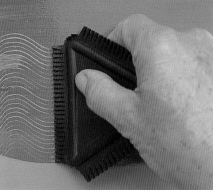

3 Take a combing implement and run it over the surface in wavy lines. Allow to dry.

1 Choose a contrasting color scheme. Apply 2–3 coats of background color.

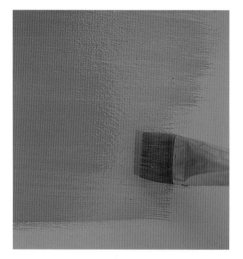

2 Add a little retarder to the contrasting color, then brush it over the basecoats.

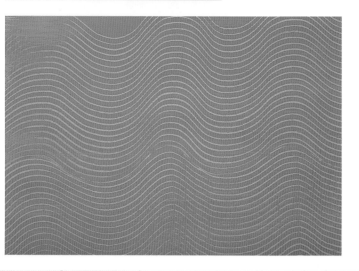

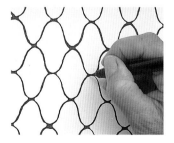

Embossing

This effect was made with structural paints. They include a set of nozzles which fit straight onto the tubes, in a similar way to a piping bag when you ice a cake.

3 Allow the paint to dry. Apply at least three coats of background paint using a 2in (5cm) brush.

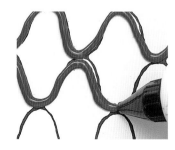

1 Trace or draw the pattern that you wish to emboss.

2 Assemble the nozzle and squeeze gently, following your tracing lines.

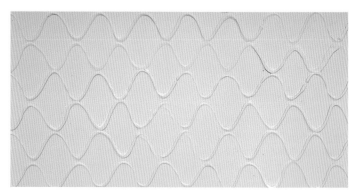

Black marble

If you enjoyed making mud-pies as a child, you will love marbling – and you won't even get your hands dirty!

2 Loosely cover with plastic foodwrap, crumpling and mixing with both hands. Tones of gray should appear where black and white blobs merge.

4 Dip the feather into white pigment and randomly repeat the movement above to create white trails marbling through the black.

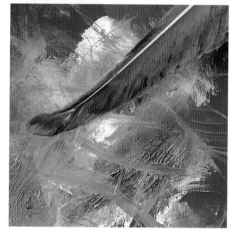

1 Apply three coats of black background. When dry, add random blobs of black and white pigment straight from the tube or bottle.

3 Remove the plastic. Draw a dampened feather diagonally across the painted surface to create a veined effect. Twist and flip the feather from side to side to blend with the damp surface. Work quickly before the paint dries.

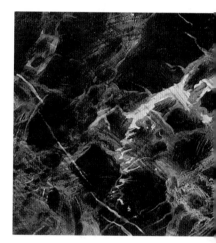

Stamping

You can buy a wide range of stamping implements. Add a little glazing medium or retarder to your chosen color to help it go on more evenly. Practice on a worksheet to get the stamp working freely before applying it to your piece.

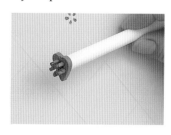

1 Paint three coats of background. When dry rule sectional lines using a chalk pencil.

2 Apply the stamp at intersections. Allow to dry.

3 Now erase the lines, but if you prefer to keep them as part of the pattern, apply two coats of spray varnish to fix them on.

Finished Effects

You can finish your decorated piece with two or three coats of varnish (see pp. 30–31), or add one of the effects shown here before applying the varnish. You could even use all three effects together. Always check the instructions on the label before using any mediums, as different brands differ in use.

Antiquing

Aging your piece will make it look more authentic.

A few of the main manufacturers list extender as retarder. Here, we use a special retarder and antiquing medium – but you can always ask your art supply store manager for advice on what products to use for the effect you are trying to achieve.

The process is disconcerting at first, but don't worry – it all comes right.

1 In a jar lid, mix a small amount of burnt umber pigment with retarder, blending well. Dip a damp brush into the mixture and paint it quickly over the surface. Don't be alarmed at the result – your design hasn't "disappeared" forever.

2 Then wipe it over with a dampened paper towel. Don't try to remove it completely.

Crackling

There are many crackling products you can buy, such as cracklure (craquelure). They are easy to apply, and the effects can vary from large to quite tiny crackles. This example uses a crackle medium which forms small crackles. Antiquing (see above) helps them to stand out more distinctly.

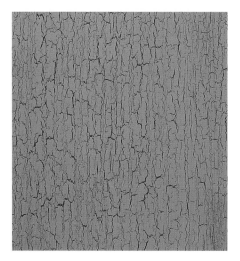

1 For an interesting background effect, simply paint the crackle medium over the piece, and allow it to dry.

2 For an interesting finished effect paint the crackle medium over the entire piece. Slowly the crackles begin to appear.

RIGHT: This kitchen work-top storage cupboard is beautifully decorated with images of vegetables and very finely-executed lettering. It has been finished with crackle glaze and antiquing medium to suit the traditional style of the decoration.

3 With a fiber-free absorbant cloth stretched over your finger, rub back in desired areas, then rub gently to feather rub the highlights. Allow to dry for several days. Wax with furniture polish to give a nice patina.

Splattering

This effect is applied with an old toothbrush. Dilute your chosen color.

1 Dip the top of the bristles into the paint. Hold the brush over a practice sheet of paper, with the bristles pointing down. Run your thumb over the bristles, moving backward from the front toward the handle. When the spray produces a fine, clean scattering of dots, you are ready to splatter your piece. Reload the brush when necessary.

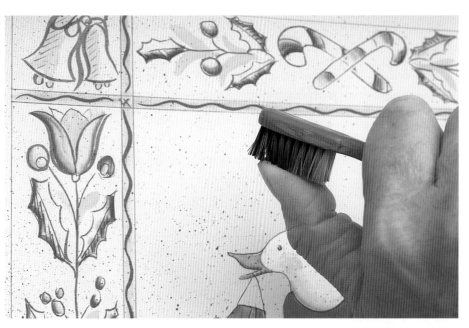

Basic Techniques

The three indispensable tools of decorative painting are the paints, the brushes and water. You, the painter, are the controller, who determines what is needed to make these components work together effectively. The following pages show you how to control your brush, and the techniques for loading it with the correct proportion of paint and water to ensure success.

Brush control

Your brush is your painting implement and needs to be harnessed and controlled sympathetically.

1 Most people find it quite comfortable to hold the brush in the cradle of the forefingers, like a pencil, with the thumb keeping it in place.

2 Avoid holding it too firmly, or at too much of a slant as shown here.

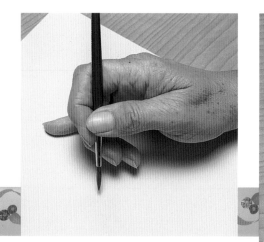

3 Before you start to paint, make sure that there are no water droplets on the brush handle or ferrule that could slide onto your work.

Movement varies according to the stroke, but generally you should aim for a loose movement from the wrist or shoulder which transfers a flowing action to the brush. To achieve balance, there must be some contact between your hand and the surface of your piece. Extending the pinkie (little finger) to act as a lever works well for some people; others find it more comfortable to tuck the pinkie in and rest on its knuckle.

4 Pull the brush hairs along with your movement, like a sleigh. Never push it like a baby carriage (pram). Aim for a steady rate of movement as you produce standard strokes. If anything, the paint flow gradually depletes as you proceed, so slowing as you tail off is better than speeding. Slowing up keeps you in better control.

The first of these strokes was painted with moderate and uniform speed; the second speeded up.

For some strokes, such as scrolls, long strokes, and curlicue embellishments, shoulder action is essential. For other strokework, resting the side of your hand on the surface and using wrist action works effectively, providing your hand is relaxed and not holding onto the brush for dear life!

Brush Loading

Brush-loading techniques determine how the brush hairs take up paint, enabling you to use the brush in the ways you choose. The aim is to work with the full range of your brush's and paint's capabilities, and if the brush is not loaded properly, the stroke produced will fall short of its potential.

The perfect stroke is one whose shape and texture conform to defined parameters, but in fact the parameters are evolving all the time. Here we build paint consistency and texture into our endeavors to show some of the better-known effects. Inventiveness is always welcome – but it is good to be aware of some general principles first.

Full loading

This is a trial-and-error exercise to enable you to get to grips with paint consistency and discover the feeling of a flowing creamy stroke.

1 Dip the brush in water. Blot out excess water. Pick up a small amount of paint. Blend it into the brush by stroking repeatedly over the same spot. This encourages the paint to be drawn up evenly through the hairs.

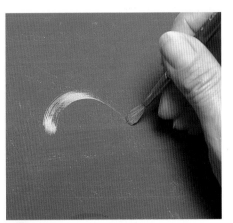

2 Now try painting a stroke. Yes, it is a failure, because the brush has insufficient paint, and perhaps too little water . . .

Loading Principles

A properly loaded brush will be able to produce a complete stroke without running out of paint. The stroke can range in texture from watery transparent to pasty opaque. The perfect texture for acrylics falls in the middle: the paint should run onto the surface as a creamy smooth opaque preparation.

Gauging the ratio of water to paint is half the battle, or rather half the fun, of decorative painting. Although manufacturers often claim that the artist can use their paints successfully straight from the tube, this is not always the case. Paints, like humans, have quirky personalities, including a tendency to be affected by weather and atmospheric conditions. This means that the ratio of water to paint may need adjustment on a daily basis.

Handle   Crimp   Ferrule   Hairs

Heel

3 Pick up the same amount of paint from the paint puddle, and blend again over the same spot as before.

4 Try and paint a stroke. This will be an improvement, but still not right. We need more paint to fill out the stroke. Loading paint into a brush must be done in stages – like adding flour to a cake mixture. Too much paint too soon will produce heavy results.

Drybrushing

Painting with very little color on the brush creates a filmy stroke in contrast to the full creamy look of full loading.

2 Make a stroke. Note that it looks wispy, as though the paint is petering out. This is a first-degree drybrushed stroke.

1 You have just painted a stroke with a fully loaded brush, so it is no longer fully loaded. Wipe the brush hairs gently against a paper towel.

5 This time we have the fullness, but the edges are ragged and dry rather than smooth and creamy. At this stage you must judge whether to pick up more paint or more water. Try a tiny amount of water first and test the result. Just dip the tip of your brush in water, and blend it on the palette over the same wet paint that you have been using. If the paint has dried up, start a new blending spot. You do not want your brush to pick up flakes of dry paint just when the formulation is nearly right.

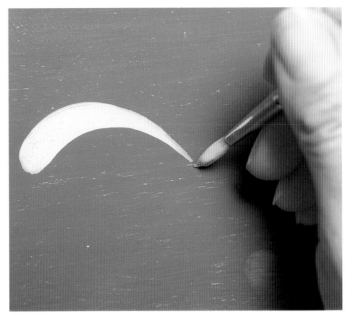

6 Try painting a stroke again. This time you should succeed in producing a creamy smooth stroke from start to finish.

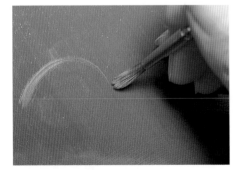

3 Wipe the brush a little more on paper towel. Paint another stroke. The stroke has become more filmy. You can, of course, wipe as much paint off the brush as you like, depending upon the effect you wish to achieve.

ABOVE: As this charming example shows, one use of drybrushing is for feather and fur effects when painting animals.

Tipping

To give the stroke a variegated look, the fully loaded brush can be tipped with one or more colors.

1 Fully load the brush as explained under "full loading" (see pp. 43–45) then just dip the very tip of the brush into your second color.

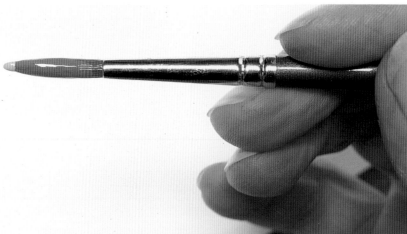

2 Only a small amount of second color is required for the subtle, variegated look you would normally wish to achieve.

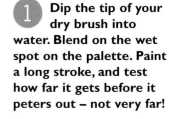

Scrolling

When you are painting longer than normal strokes, such as scrolls and other embellishments, you need more water to carry the paint farther.

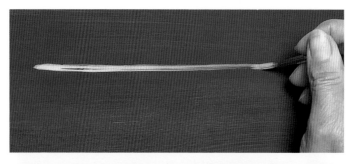

1 Dip the tip of your dry brush into water. Blend on the wet spot on the palette. Paint a long stroke, and test how far it gets before it peters out – not very far!

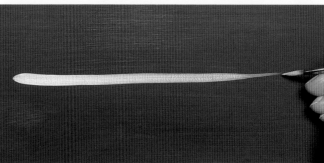

2 Pick up some more paint. Blend. Dip the brush in water. Blend again. Paint a long stroke. The consistency is now sufficiently fluid to create an extended stroke without being too watery.

This is a familiar decorative style from the Stuttgart region of Germany. The large flowers are painted in bold comma and S strokes, tipped with white to create a more interesting variegated effect. The smaller florals in contrasting colors, also tipped, help to produce a pleasing balanced design.

③ This produces a variegated look. Tip the brush with two colors for a multicolored version.

Round brush versus flat brush

These exercises were demonstrated with a round brush, but a flat brush could be used equally well. For the sideloading and double loading techniques that follow, however, the flat brush is more appropriate. Some adept painters use a round brush for every technique, flattening the hairs between their fingers for side and double loading. This is something for you to experiment with.

Undermixing

Many images are not a solid color but are composed of undermixed – or more correctly, under blended – colors.

② Then roll it on the palette – not too much, but just enough to marble the paint.

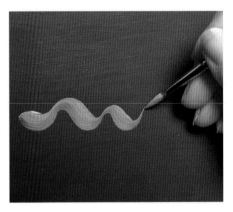

③ This is a useful technique if you do not want the paint to look too solid.

① Fully load the brush. Tip it with another color.

Sideloading

Sideloading is a revelation for most beginners, and one of the peak experiences of learning decorative painting. It creates an amazing look that graduates from a solid color into a sublime nothingness. Two techniques are utilized in conjunction to achieve the effect. The first is balancing the ratio of water and paint to obtain the right consistency; and the second, which gives the stroke its unique character, is the control over the paint distribution on the brush. Follow the procedure here using a flat brush with long hairs, such as a shader, to hold the full complement of paint and water required to complete a stroke.

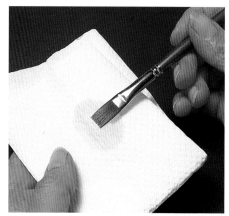

1 **Dip the brush in water. Note that the brush looks shiny because it is full of water.**

2 **Place one side of the wet brush against a folded paper towel. As soon as the hairs on the upper side lose their sheen, lift the brush up, because this signals that the water content is about right to begin the sideloading procedure.**

3 **Dip one corner of the brush into the paint puddle.**

Double loading

Double loading follows the same method as sideloading, except that the brush is loaded with two colors, one on each corner, to give a two-tone but subtly blended effect.

1 **Dampen the brush and blot, as for sideloading. Load the brush with a different color on each corner of the bristle tip.**

2 **The colors merge subtly in the middle as you make a stroke on your practice paper to take off the excess paint before you make your stroke on the surface you are painting.**

4 Begin stroking the brush back and forth over a small strip of no more than an inch (2.5 cm). The paint is drawing up into the hairs. Next we want it to encourage the paint to spread across the hairs in a graduated tone – strong to weak. Begin walking the brush fractional steps to the right and then to the left. When you move left, only go far enough to encourage distribution and graduation of color. You will see it happening before your eyes.

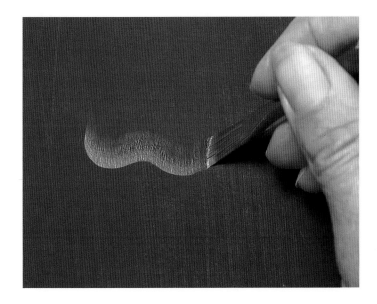

5 After all this blending on the palette, the distribution should be right, but have you got enough paint and water in the brush to complete a stroke? Probably not. So dip the tip of the non-painted corner into water. Blot — only a touch. Blend. Now, paint the stroke.

3 The trick is to walk the brush just far enough to the left or right to encourage a gentle blending, but not so far that the colors overlap and mix too much.

Strokes

With a few basic strokes, you can create countless motifs – and paint in some renowned strokework styles. Beginning strokework is like learning to print the letters of the alphabet and then stringing them together into words. At first the letters can be misshapen or inconsistent in size, but with practice you become adept at marshaling them correctly. The same thing happens with stroke painting shapes: the building blocks of decorative art.

When you are reasonably confident with a basic stroke, you can modify it slightly to produce a new look. A ruffled flower petal, for example, might look impossible to paint – until you discover that it is only a crescent stroke with a few wobbles. This section shows the basic strokes, with their variations, and the brushes used to paint them. Step-by-step illustrations explain how each stroke is painted, and demonstrate how you can apply it to create different designs.

1 The wooden end of the paintbrush was dipped in paint and then stamped on the paper to produce a succession of dots of decreasing size.

2 Dipping a pencil eraser into paint produces a series of diminishing dots.

3 A stylus is used here. The homemade variety would consist of a straight pin stuck into a pencil eraser. The pin head is similar in size to a stylus. Both produce a line of small dots.

Rainbow Dots

This pattern is built up by a series of graduated dots. The brush is refreshed with a new color after the fifth dot.

Dotwork

It may seem odd to begin an exploration of painting with dots, but they provide such encouragement, showing how easy and rewarding it is to create colorful patterns.

The instrument you choose is optional. The wooden end of your paintbrush is perhaps the handiest! Whatever the implement, the technique of simply dipping it into paint and then stamping it onto a surface provides plenty of scope for enchanting creations.

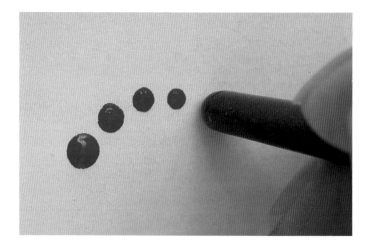

1 Dip the wooden end of a brush into red paint. One dip will make a succession of approximately 5–6 graduated dots. Apply the dots in an arch.

Floral Dot Border

To create dots of a uniform size, as in the case of these petals, the end of a brush or stylus is dipped for each dot application.

1 Make the flower's center with a yellow dot. Wipe the end of the brush and dip it in blue, placing dots evenly around the central yellow dot.

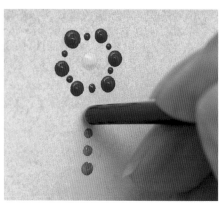

2 Use a stylus to fill in between each petal with smaller blue dots. You could choose a different color for these if you wanted. Use the wooden end of a brush to make the stem. Dot from the bottom in graduated sizes, from large to small, to finish at the top of the stem.

3 Now dot the leaves at 45° from the base of the stem. These are also graduated dots. You can repeat these florals side by side to make an attractive border. You probably realize that the pattern variations you might create by this method are endless.

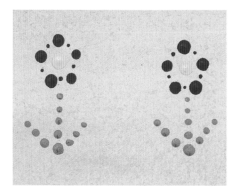

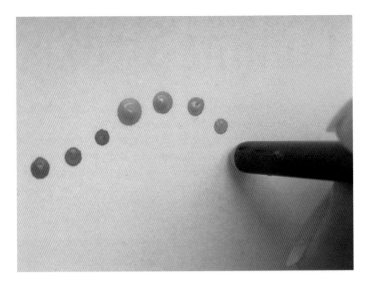

2 Remove any red paint left on the end of the brush and repeat, using orange, this time curving in the opposite direction. Wipe off the orange, and then dip in yellow and repeat.

3 Green comes after yellow in the rainbow, followed by blue. Continue with each color in the same manner.

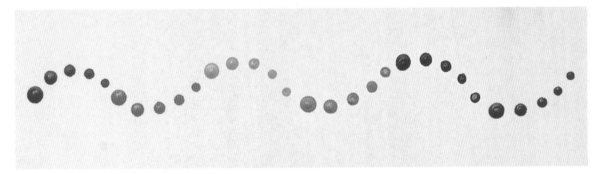

4 This attractive dotwork rainbow border could be continued to any length and used effectively in a child's bedroom.

Eraser Dots

Eraser dots are perfect for creating bunches of grapes. The solid and ghosted dot combinations suggest lighting effects.

1 *Dip the eraser end into paint and begin stamping dots to make a cluster that tails off, as shown. As the paint depletes, the ghosted effect increases.*

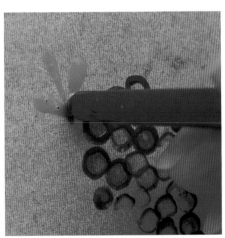

2 *Use the wooden end of the brush to suggest vine leaves. To produce this effect, stamp a dot onto the surface but before you lift off, drag the brush toward the bunch of grapes to pull some of the paint away from the dot.*

3 *Make another bunch of grapes with the pencil eraser, varying the shape and textures from the first example. With the wooden end of a brush, paint some leaves, at a different angle from the first example. Place some dot patterns and a few light squiggle strokes as tendrils on the background to liven up the design.*

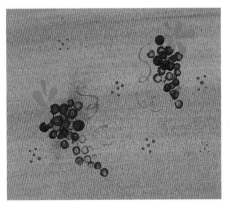

1 Press the round brush to flatten out the hairs into a rounded shape.
2 Pull the stroke into a gentle curve, releasing pressure as you pull.
3 Slow down as the stroke tails off, so the hairs can realign. Lift the brush cleanly.
The fat end of the stroke is referred to as the "head," and the thin end as the "tail."

Comma Stroke

The comma is the most fundamental stroke. Its shape is a natural complement of the round brush. As you press the tip down onto the surface, it flattens into the head of the comma. Then pull the brush toward you in a gentle arc, gradually releasing pressure so that the hairs realign as the stroke tails off. With practice, you will be able to paint commas starting from all directions.

The Daisy

To ensure that the flower will look balanced once painted, sketch an ellipse with a chalk pencil to act as a guideline. Place a dot one third of the way down from the top midpoint of the ellipse. Begin your comma strokes on the outer edge, finishing on the dot. Paint the commas in pair opposites.

1 Paint the first pair of comma strokes. Remember to hold the brush upright to the surface, using your pinkie (little finger) to balance – either fully extended or tucked under, in which case the lower joint becomes the balancing point.

VARIATION • I

Heart Border

To paint a basic heart shape, put two comma stroke tails together, as shown.

1 *Paint two comma strokes, one from the left and one from the right, with the tails butted next to each other.*

2 *Just below the point of the heart, add the green commas in pairs, as shown; then the yellow commas. Repeat Steps 1 and 2 to complete the required length of your border.*

3 *This pattern will look pretty on a kitchen or bedroom wall or shade (blind) – as a horizontal or a vertical design.*

② **Now paint the second pair of commas. Turn your work if necessary to find a comfortable direction in which to paint.**

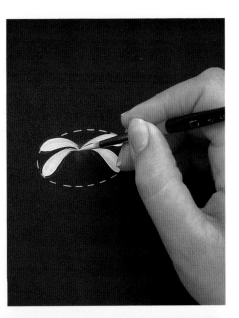

③ **With two pairs of petals complete, fill in with two more comma stroke pairs at the top and bottom, as shown. Note that the top pair is shorter to give a natural perspective to the flower.**

④ **Where the tails meet in the center, put a yellow dot with the wooden end of the brush. Add a few comma stroke leaves to each side of your flower head design.**

VARIATION • 2

Tulip

When you put comma stroke heads together, as shown here, you form a tulip blossom.

1 *Outline a faint design of three tulips (see p. 121) in chalk. For each blossom, paint two comma stroke petals with the tails pointed outward.*

2 *Add comma stroke leaves, graduating down in size for a "natural" look. Do not feel too restricted by the chalk guidelines since this will spoil the flow of the stroke. Now you can add a simple line for each stem, using a liner brush.*

3 *Finish with comma strokes at the center of each blossom for the feathery stamens. The larger flowers have a few more stamens than the smaller ones.*

Broadside

1 Set the brush down in an upright stance on the chisel edge, that is the tip of the bristles.

2 Begin to apply pressure, using the flat plane, or broadside, of the bristles, and pull the brush toward you to make a straight broadside stroke.

3 Remember to return to the chisel edge of the brush before ending the stroke and lifting off the surface.

This stroke uses a flat brush and gets its name from the flat plane of the brush, known as the broadside. Expertise with the flat brush involves swiveling between the broadside and the narrow side, which is called the chisel.

1 **Start with the center stroke in turquoise. On either side, paint two yellow strokes the same length.**

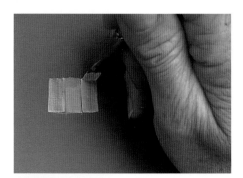

Navajo Design

This simple but attractive design is based on the geometric style of decoration used by Native American Navajos. Here, vibrant contrasting colors were used, which would be perfect for a wall border motif in a child's room, or even as a border on a window shade (blind), or lampshade, for the kitchen or bathroom.
You must plan even a simple design like this before you start.

2 **Paint two more yellow strokes on each side, as shown. Add a short yellow stroke to the top. Finish with stepped blocks in a red-brown, such as raw sienna.**

Checkerboard Design

This pattern is good practice for alternating between the broadside and the chisel. At first sight, you might think it was produced only on the broadside, but as you paint it, you will find that the chisel acts as a stabilizer between each broadside stroke.

I *Paint the outside border using a round or liner brush.*

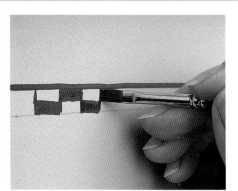

2 *Then paint the border, using a flat brush. Slide down on the chisel and across on the broadside in repeat formation.*

3 *Fill the unpainted squares on the second row with broadside strokes – here we have used yellow to contrast with the red.*

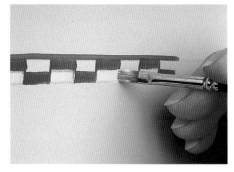

Chisel Stroke

You would not normally paint on the chisel. A liner brush does a better job! The chisel stroke is a connecting movement, and an integral part of a broadside stroke.

1 The chisel stroke uses the chisel edge (tip) of the brush to paint a line. Set down onto the surface in an upright stance.

2 Slide the chisel edge along to make a clean, thin stroke.

3 Or, make a smudge line effect by scribbling to the left and right very slightly.

Zigzag

The zigzag pattern is a clean and attractive movement. Zigzag designs are evident in most cultures; this border is similar to an Aztec design.

2 Add a few dots made with the wooden handle of the brush to finish the design effect.

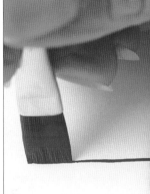

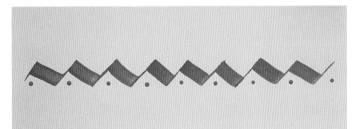

1 The zigzag pattern rises on the chisel and falls on the broadside, the chisel acting as a connecting movement.

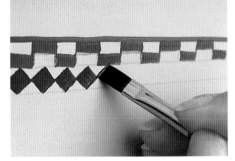

4 *Once the border is complete, start the checkerboard design with the brush at a 45° angle. Down on the broadside; slide into position for next check on the chisel; repeat.*

5 *After each row of black checks use a brush loaded with white paint and repeat the same movement as Step 4 to fill in the white checks.*

Continue Steps 4 and 5 until your checkerboard is complete.

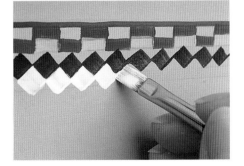

6 *As a finishing touch, place a dot in the corner of your board with the wooden end of a brush, as shown.*

Techniques in context

Beautiful designs often depend upon simple strokes, alone or in combination. The basic comma stroke, in particular, features widely in even the most accomplished floral works.

Pansy Trio

Onya Tolmasoff

A medium-toned background has been used in this painting – unusual for leaf and floral motifs, which generally place light tones against darker ones. You can see the comma stroke used well here, and some tipped strokes were applied for contrast. This design is painted in the Russian "Zhostovoy" style.

Slavic Wall Plate

Lana Williams

This plate is painted almost exclusively in comma strokes – a perfect example of how mastery of one stroke can open up a world of exciting patterns for you to paint.

Luminous Roses

Martha Kenton

The perfect design for the colorist who loves to paint traditional multipetaled roses. A flat brush was double and triple loaded to combine comma, chisel and crescent strokes. (See pp. 70–73 for crescent strokes.) Values were introduced by a gradual layering of color glazes.

Decorated Chest

Sidney Barnsley

This impressive chest was decorated by Sidney Barnsley, one of the key personalities of the Arts and Crafts Movement in England in the late 1800s. With a deliberately limited palette and a unique sense of movement, it is a most appealing work. The juxtaposition of commas, crescents and S strokes is also refreshingly original. (See pp. 66–67 for S stroke.)

1 Set the flat brush down in an upright stance, applying pressure to the broadside.

2 Pull the stroke round and toward you, releasing pressure as you come up onto the chisel.

3 Tail off in a sliding motion on the chisel.

Flat Comma

The flat comma generally begins at the head or blunt end, but your decision to start forming the stroke at the tail or the blunt end will depend upon whether you are right- or left-handed.

Right-handers should follow the instructions shown on the left. A left-hander will make the flat comma in the opposite direction.

An alternative to the flat comma is the scroll, which begins at the bottom of the stroke on the chisel edge of the brush. Slide the chisel along, keeping the brush upright. Increase pressure as you come into a curve, presenting the broadside of the brush. Gently draw up onto the chisel to make a clean ending.

Leaf Sprigs

This pretty design can act as a basis for many of the floral decorations you may want to create.

As noted above, whether you begin the flat comma or scroll strokes at the blunt or tail end will usually depend on if you are right- or left-handed, but practice and go for what feels most comfortable to you to determine the direction of the stroke.

1 Paint a leaf on the left side. Use a flat comma stroke if you're right-handed; a scroll, if you're left-handed.

Floral Border

Now use the leaf sprigs to create a pretty border, integrating the strokes you have learned so far.

2 *Add interest with a zigzag line, using the broadside and chisel combination shown on page 57. Add dots on either side of your flower, using the wooden tip of the brush.*

3 *This motif makes a very effective border. Repeat Steps 1 and 2 to the required length.*

1 *Paint a leaf sprig as featured above. Then with a round or liner brush, paint a series of diminishing-sized commas to form a flower.*

2 Paint the second comma or scroll above the first leaf, as shown.

3 Repeat for the third leaf, making sure that the downward stroke of the tail blends into those of the first and second leaves. Remember to lift off cleanly at the end of each stroke.

4 Follow the same procedure for the other side, using a darker tone of paint. If you're right-handed, the scroll movement is easier; for left-handers, the flat comma movement is easier.

VARIATION • 2

Flat Comma and Scroll Border

Another simple, charming border uses a combination of flat comma and ordinary comma strokes in contrasting colors, with scroll strokes in the opposite direction.

3 *Paint a series of three blue comma strokes under the arches of the flat comma strokes.*

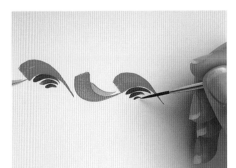

2 *Paint a green comma stroke on the cradle of the scroll strokes, as shown.*

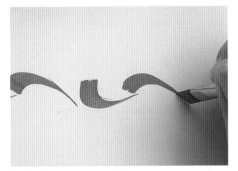

1 *Paint a series of flat commas and scrolls placed in opposite formation.*

1 With a flat brush placed horizontally on the surface, apply some pressure, pulling the brush away.

2 After a short distance, begin gently rotating the brush in a clockwise direction.

3 As you come onto the chisel, twist the stroke off.

Leaf Floral

Simple motifs like this are often used as fillers in a larger design.

Leaf Stroke

As its name suggests, the leaf stroke is ideal for depicting leaves quickly. With practice you will be able to produce this stroke with a rapid twirl of the brush! Begin on the broadside, then as you pull on the stroke, rotate the brush slightly between your thumb and forefinger in a clockwise direction, lifting onto the chisel as you make the movement. It is like twisting the stroke off.

1 Draw a star with three intersecting lines, evenly spaced. Begin painting leaf strokes in each section of the star. Note that the green paint was tipped with bronze (see pp. 48–49) to produce a more interesting effect.

2 With the wooden end of a brush, add four blue dots. Finish with a dotted yellow center.

Leaf Garland

Using this stroke, you can create a quick leafy floral garland.

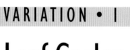

I *With a chalk pencil, draw a gently curving arch. Apply leaf strokes in a balanced distribution along its length.*

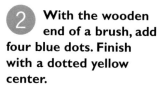

2 *As contrast, use a liner brush to intersperse some smaller comma strokes. To enliven the garland, add some dot-style florals.*

3 *A garland can be as simple or detailed as you like. Perhaps you would like to experiment with this design, adding a few more florals and ornaments.*

Pivot Leaf

This leaf variation can be used to construct heart-shaped leaves. Create them by placing the flat side of two pivot leaf strokes side by side. Or you can simply use one stroke by itself.

1 Begin on the chisel, which is held at right angles to the body.
2 The bulge is going to be on the right, so that the leading edge should be on the right-hand side of the chisel. Apply pressure, pivoting the stroke around in a clockwise direction.
3 As you rotate, the brush comes around and up onto the chisel again – just before it is fully upright, pull down into a slight tail.

Pivot Leaf Heart

This heart design is constructed with two plump pivot leaf strokes for the heart itself and single long pivot strokes for the leaf decoration.

1 Paint half a heart, with the bulge to the left. In this case, the leading edge of the chisel as it rotates will be to the left. Paint the other half on the right. Imagine the heart painted in green instead of red, and you will see how much it resembles a leaf.

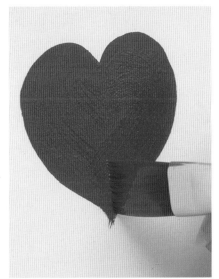

2 Decorate the heart with pivot leaf strokes along the top. Pull out the tail of each stroke. Add some yellow dots to suggest florals. A stylus was used to add some accents in the center of the flowers.

VARIATION • I

Hearts and flowers

Heart designs can be used to decorate many items, such as trinket or jewelry boxes, or even chests used to store momentos.

I *Paint your heart using pivot leaf strokes. Although red has been used here you can experiment with different colors.*

2 *Add a cascade of flowers on top using comma, dot and leaf strokes. To balance the design add a base of flat comma and scroll strokes.*

3 *The final motif would make an attractive central design – perhaps with a simple border of line or dots.*

1 Load a flat brush and set down on the surface. Begin to apply pressure.

2 As you turn the brush in an arch gently move the brush in a single, flowing ruffled stroke — a steady, even pressure is the key for a good final effect.

3 As you come to the end of the arch, lift off cleanly.

Ruffled Leaf

This stroke is a variation of the ordinary leaf and pivot leaf strokes. It is produced in the same way as its sister strokes, but the brush is jiggled slightly to create their characteristic ruffled look. Two stroke opposites are painted side by side to make a rounded leaf with a fluted edge. Vary the amount of pressure as you go into the stroke depending upon whether you want a rounded leaf that tapers off quickly, or a long, narrow one that gradually forms a point. Although the stroke is intended for leaves, you can sometimes adapt it to other images.

Ruffled Flowers

This design shows how the ruffled leaf stroke can be used for flower petals as well as leaves. It also shows that the stroke can form leaves of varying length and can be used as the edge stroke around the leaf only.

1 Using a flat brush paint the edge of each leaf using a ruffled leaf stroke in an arch. Vary the length and width of each leaf. Before the paint dries, get a damp brush and blend in the paint to fill the center of the leaf.

VARIATION • 1

Black-eyed Susan

The petals are pivot leaf strokes, made plump by extra pressure going into the stroke. The leaves are ruffled leaf strokes, given their sleek appearance by not applying too much pressure and gradually tapering off to a point.

2 *Repeat in the same way, placing pivot strokes at right angles to each other, as shown.*

3 *Create the dark center with the wooden end of your brush. Place two red comma strokes around the center.*

1 *Pencil an X on the surface, and paint a pivot stroke in one section.*

2 Load a liner brush with a darker tone of green and paint in the leaf veins, starting with the center vein. Then, add a few thinner veins branching out from the center vein — tapering to the end of each stroke.

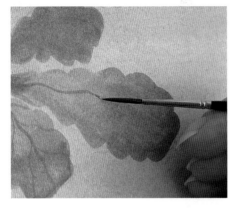

3 Draw a chalk design for each of the flowers. Base in the petals and center of each flower (see pp. 96–97) in cream. For the petals base in using the ruffled leaf stroke. Add green shading around the center of the flower and petals, see the final picture for reference.

4 Add stems with a liner brush loaded with a dark-toned green. Build up the flowers with white using a small flat brush.

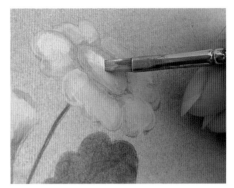

5 Add a wash of yellow to the center of each flower (see pp. 100–101).

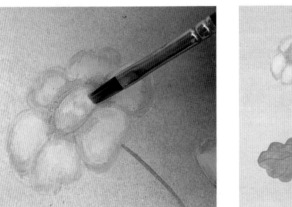

4 *Paint ruffled leaf strokes to form the left-hand side of the three leaves, positioned as shown.*

5 *Add the right-hand half of each leaf, again using the ruffled leaf stroke. Take care that the tails of each stroke butt up together so that the tips end clean.*

6 *The border is a combination of alternating flat strokes and commas.*

1 Here a round brush is being used. Hold the brush upright, lightly skimming the surface in a gentle curving motion while applying more pressure.

2 Keep up the pressure at midpoint; reverse direction before starting to release pressure.

3 Slow down to tail off the stroke neatly as the hairs realign. Lift cleanly.

Ropes and Ribbons

Flat brushes can also be used to make S strokes. For the rope design, begin with a flat brush, on a short chisel slide, shifting to the broadside on the S bend, and then shifting back again onto the chisel while tailing off.

The ribbons are painted with a round brush and the S strokes are not uniform. This gives a flowing, "unraveled" effect.

S Stroke

This graceful stroke begins and ends on the tip of the brush. Pressure is applied going into the curve and released coming out of it. S strokes can be painted in various sizes, thicknesses and lengths. They can be perfectly symmetrical, as they are in the rope design, or gently suggest an S shape, as seen in the leaves of the bluebell image. Connecting a series of S strokes creates a ribbon effect, as used in the guitar strap.

ROPE

(1) **Draw two faint parallel lines in pencil as a guide for the width of the rope. Using a flat brush, paint an S stroke. Then begin the second stroke from the top of the first stroke.**

(2) **Remember to leave a slight gap between the fatter sections of the strokes. Repeat the uniform S stroke formation to desired length.**

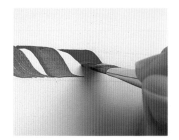

Bluebell Sprigs

Floral sprigs are fun to paint: So many flowers can be constructed from a series of S strokes for the petals, stems and leaves. Here is a simple bluebell motif.

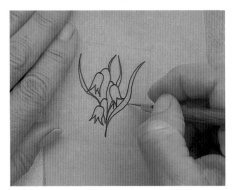

1 *Although simple sprigs can be painted freehand, you may find it easier to trace a pattern (see p. 121).*

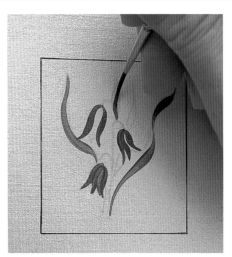

2 *Paint the leaves, using a very rough, elongated type of S stroke instead of being too precise. Then paint the two outer petals of the bluebell blossoms, using S strokes.*

3 *Finish with the center petal, trying to make sure that the three blue S strokes merge where they meet, so that a true bell shape is made for each flower.*

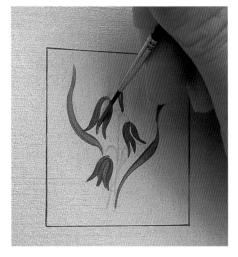

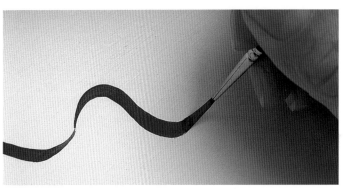

3 As a variation, you can alternate the choice of color for the strokes. For an interesting aged effect, rub over the rope design lightly with a scrunched piece of paper when the paint is dry.

2 From the tail of the first stroke, add another S stroke, but this time make it a slightly different length and thickness – even change direction – to give the effect of flowing material.

RIBBON

1 Using a thin brush, paint an S stroke of any length you wish.

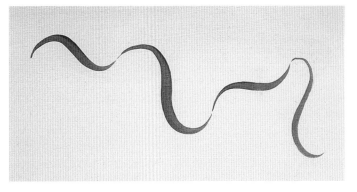

3 The purpose of this combination of thick and thin S strokes is to make the ribbon design look graceful as it "unravels" across your chosen surface.

VARIATION • 2

Guitar

This guitar looks solid, yet it is made up of a number of flowing S strokes.

3 *The strings are lightly suggested with six imprecise liner strokes.*

I *Trace the pattern from p. 121. Fill in the body first. The dark brown riser was painted with two overlapping S strokes, using a flat brush. The stem and front are based in white and chestnut before the tracing is reapplied.*

2 *After you have retraced the fine details onto the body of the guitar you can add the strap. Here the ribbon type S stroke is painted with a round brush. Add the details of the stem. The hole is based in (see pp. 96–97).*

Techniques in context

Scrolls, leaf strokes (used for leaves and hearts) and S strokes are all exhibited here in a strikingly varied array of designs and applications to inspire you and capture your imagination for future projects.

Hand Mirror with Flowers

Onya Tolmasoff

Most if not all countries have their distinctive decorative styles. This example imitates a Russian approach to florals known as "Zhostovo." It uses S and comma strokes over a dark background, which sets off the beauty and texture of the strokework. The strokes were painted wet-on-wet – one over another that had not yet dried.

A Lovely Summer Morning

Priscilla Hauser

A beautifully unusual application of acrylic gouache on a galvanized watering can, by the well-known American painter Priscilla Hauser. Her expertise at sideloading (see pp. 102–103 and 108–109) is also evident.

   Floral designs like this also show pivot leaf and ruffled crescent strokes to great effect.

Large Shallow Bowl (detail)

Rhonda Thorne

Rosemaling, which is characterized by scrolls and long liner strokes, is a style of decorative painting associated with Scandinavia. Control is the key to this approach. The artist must be able to paint with smooth, sweeping movements from the shoulder.

   Crescent strokes are also used to good effect here (see pp. 70–73.)

Floral Designs

Lana Williams

This night table is painted with basic strokes: commas, S strokes and dipped crescents. The dots are subdued but effective. Some of the S strokes are applied alongside each other and lined with darker tones. Painted on stained wood in traditional colors, this would fit most environments.

Tray in Rogaland-style Rosemaling

Kate Mellor

This symmetrical painting style is a Norwegian form of rosemaling, known as Rogaland. Long strokes and scrolls are its main features, but closer examination reveals the presence of other strokes, such as commas and crescents.

St. Nick's Chocolate Kisses Box

Prudy E. Vannier

Long liner strokes are the main theme here. Note the heart-shaped tree decorations made with leaf pivot strokes. The ribbons were produced with solid color, using S strokes and crescents.

Crescent Stroke

The name of this stroke suggests its shape. Crescents can be painted as slight or more extreme curves. They can curve inward or outward. Both round and flat brushes can be used to produce the shapes. The example in the panel is painted with a flat brush.

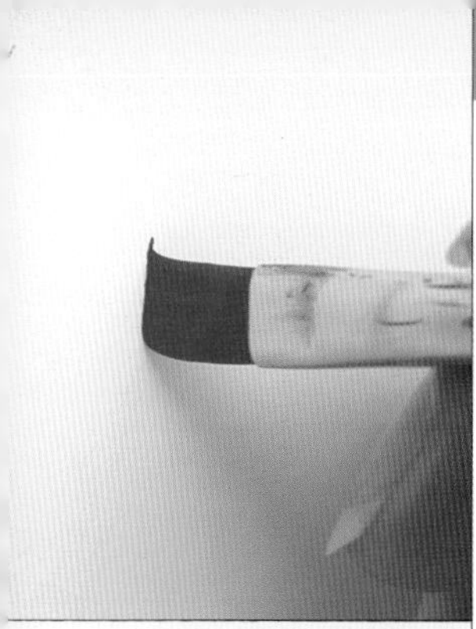

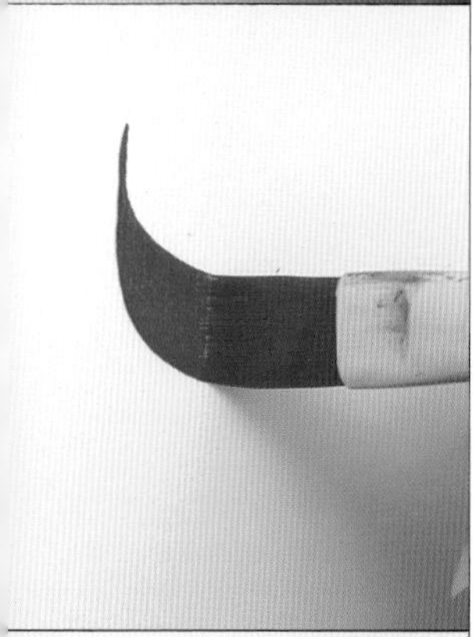

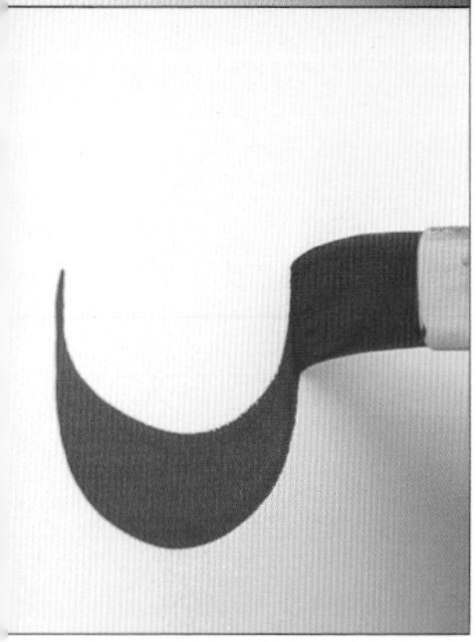

1 With the brush on the chisel, pull it slightly toward you but mindful of the fact that you will soon apply pressure to the right.

2 While pulling the stroke toward you, gradually apply pressure to the right as you go into a gentle curve on the broadside. When you arrive at midpoint, be aware that you must begin releasing pressure as the stroke moves into the upward section of the curve.

3 Gradually release pressure on the upward curve coming up onto the chisel. Lift cleanly.

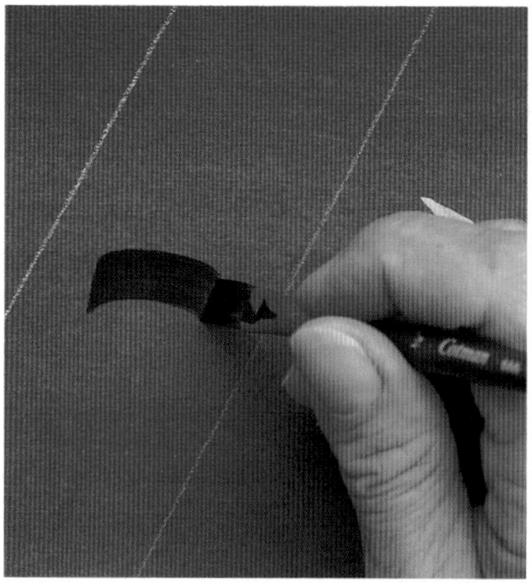

1 Paint a flat, slightly arched crescent, beginning and ending on the broadside of the brush. The next stroke will be a dipped crescent, exactly the same and overlapping the first stroke.

Moon, Boat and Fish

The crescents in this design were painted with a flat brush, some beginning and ending on the broadside and others on the chisel.

VARIATION • 1

Swimming Fish

Dipped crescents can be used to great decorative effect as scales.

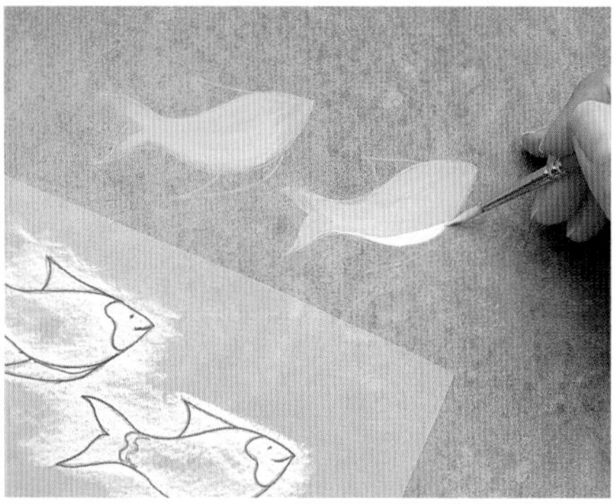

1 *Paint two coats of green wash (see pp. 100–101) for the background. Before the second coat is dry random rag drop (see p. 35) to create an effect of light shining through the water.*

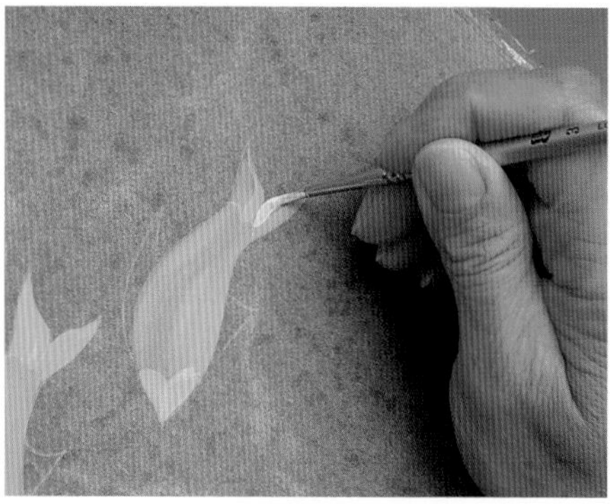

2 *Once the body and tail have been based in, use a small round brush to paint the head and tail sections. Use comma strokes to contour the shape you are filling.*

3 *Fill in the dorsal and underside fins with a contrasting color.*

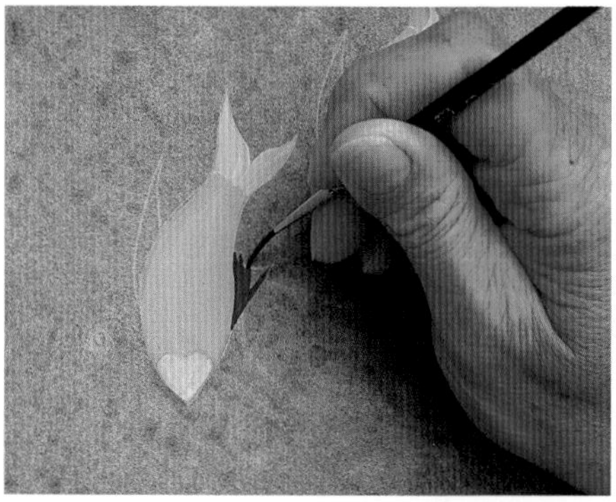

2 The moon crescent, tapered at each end, begins and ends on the chisel. The nose protrusion is painted with a much smaller crescent. Note that the main fish stroke is also a tapered crescent.

3 The pale blue areas on the fish are created with three comma strokes. The tails of two comma strokes make the tail section of the fish; one comma stroke is applied at the head section and tails off under the body. Dot the eye. The boat's sail is a broadside crescent.

4 The border is a simple rope design made with a series of S strokes, using a small round brush. Draw a chalk line to act as your guide.

5 Sparkles on the water and a starlit night keep the boat on course. Small fleck suggestions with a liner brush are all that's needed; the same for the ripples created by the jumping fish. Give the moon face a little suggestion of a mouth.

4 *The strokes demarcating the head and tail region from the main body are made with dipped crescent strokes painted with a round brush.*

5 *The scales are dipped crescents painted with a flat brush. Begin at the head and paint across in rows from head to tail. Iridescent paint was used to accentuate the scales.*

6 *To give the impression of underwater activity and the presence of other life, add a few S strokes, using a round brush loaded with a dark tone.*

1 The stroke begins like the ordinary crescent, but immediately it begins to arch, introduce a flutter into your painting action.

2 As you are painting the arched section, the flutters can be regular or irregular.

3 The brush swings onto the chisel as pressure is released. Lift the brush off cleanly.

Ruffled Petal Floral

Many flowers appear to be composed of a series of ruffled petals, whether in a single layer or several. The ruffled crescent can therefore create quite an authentic look.

Other Crescents

Crescent variations can add subtle effects to many floral designs. The arched section of a ruffled crescent wavers to give petals a fluttering look, and the tall tapers of the elongated crescent introduces the impression of shading (see the variation below).

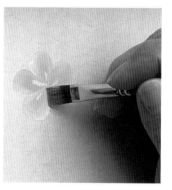

1 Sketch some guidelines for the placement of five petals. If you think of a stick man with outstretched head, arms and legs, this will help. They should line up with the center of each petal.

Dogwood Rose

The elongated crescent is so subtle that it's barely noticeable unless you know where to look! See how delicately it's done in step 4.

1 *Sketch in some guidelines and begin painting the petals so that their midpoint coincides with the markers.*

2 *With a light yellow tone, fill in the center where the lower arch of each crescent converges.*

3 *Pick up a pale yellow tone on your finger. Dab it on the palette to dispel excess paint. Use it now to apply a hazy yellow effect.*

4 Use your finger to dab a light green tone into the flower center. When it is dry, dab in very pale yellow. Then use a stylus to add a few dots of medium brown.

2 Fill in the center where the underside arches converge, then add the leaves, using ruffled leaf strokes. Each leaf is made up of two strokes with the flat sides facing.

3 A double loaded brush with medium and dark green tones for the leaves creates a varied effect. Add the sepals with a liner brush.

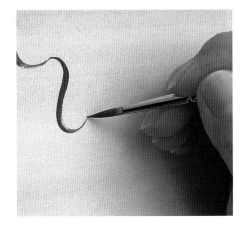

5 With a round brush, paint two S strokes to suggest a ribbon trailing away from the flower.

5 *The leaves are created with double loaded ruffles, as in the previous example. With a liner brush, pick up a slightly lighter tone than the leaf and add veins.*

4 *Pick up a miniscule speck of medium-toned paint on the corner of a flat brush. Blend on the palette. Shade around the outer area of the center section. Pick up a slightly darker tone on the corner of your brush and paint the elongated crescents, as illustrated, onto each petal.*

6 *As an illustration of how you can build onto a pattern, rosebuds are added, along with some trailing ribbons, and all enclosed in a simple border.*

1 Hold a flat brush just above the ferrule between the thumb and forefinger. It must be perpendicular. The leading edge will form the outside of the circle while it pivots around the central point.

2 The circle is nearly half complete. You might find your other hand useful to steady the movement by holding the top of your brush with it, guiding the brush as it twirls.

3 The circle now closes in with a final wedge-shaped gap yet to be filled. You can go around for a second and third time if you like.

Canal Boat Rose

In the late 18th and early 19th centuries in Britain, a unique decorative art style developed, featuring roses and castles. Just about every object, including the canal boat itself, was boldly decorated with these images.

Circles

With the twirl of a brush you can make a circle. Circles are useful in creating quick impressions of round images, such as fruit, as the backing for some florals, such as the English canal boat rose, or for more unusual images like ladybugs (ladybirds).

① **Paint the base circle. Then, in a darker tone, paint a smaller circle to represent the darkened part of the flower's center.**

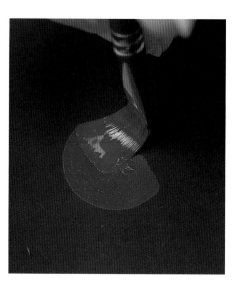

VARIATION • 1

Ladybug

This design is great fun! Remember your fascination when you first saw a ladybug (ladybird). A red bug with black spots, and a friendly bug at that!

2 Using a liner brush loaded with black paint, follow the chalk lines traced on in the previous step. Paint two comma strokes with the tails meeting in the middle for the black head section. Use S strokes for the appendages.

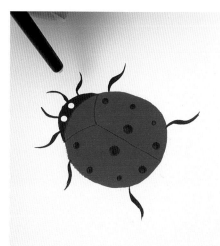

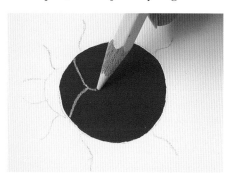

1 Trace the ladybug onto the surface. Using the circle stroke, paint the main body in bright red. Then trace on the main body lines with a chalk pencil.

3 With the wooden end of the brush, dot the spots and the eyes with black and white colors as illustrated.

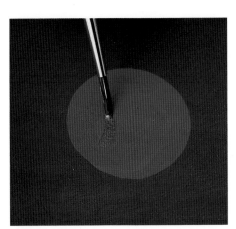

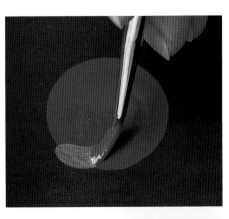

3 Now begin painting a series of four comma strokes, one on top of the other, beginning at the top left-hand side. Each stroke tails to the right. Then start the same process from the right.

2 Place the first comma stroke, hugging the darkened center space, as shown.

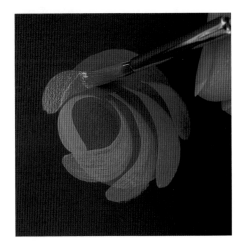

4 Paint three comma strokes on the right, with their tails scissoring between those on the left.

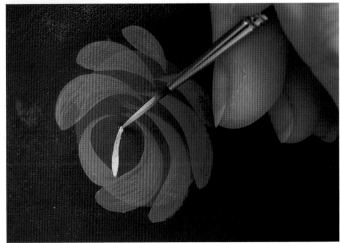

5 Add a few paddle strokes in yellow for the stamens — three or four should be enough, see the final picture for reference.

VARIATION • 2

Chrysanthemum

The same movement is used to create the base circle for this chrysanthemum, but in a less disciplined way with an underloaded brush.

2 *Load a flat brush with undermixed paint and then tip it with white. Paint a few flat comma and scroll strokes. Add more strokes to fill out the corolla. Touch the flower center with a tiny amount of yellow.*

3 *Add the stem and leaves, using the flat drybrush technique, see p. 46–47.*

1 *Base in the suggestion of a circle to create a drybrushed look. Darken the tone around the base of the circle.*

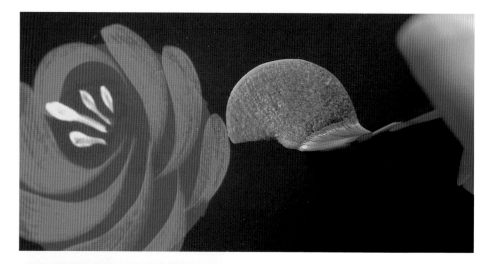

6 At the base of your flower add rose leaves formed of pivot leaf strokes (see p. 63), with a small "tail" as the tip of each leaf.

7 The classic canal boat rose can be used on its own as a single motif on an object or with any number of other simplified floral designs.

VARIATION • 3

Tree of Life

The tree of life is a universal symbol of renewal and is familiar in many versions. This design is remarkably simple and effective, and the round orange strokes fill it with vibrancy. The simple leaf strokes are casually applied. Stroke suggestion rather than stroke perfection is the aim here, so just relax as you twist off those leaf strokes. This is the joyous aspect of decorative art – careful stroke practice to begin with, but once you are confident, you can become more impressionistic.

1 Base in the tree trunk, painting from top to bottom and allowing your strokes to tail off. Using the guideline for the crown of the tree, paint leaf strokes around the periphery and then fill in the center in a medium tone of green. Paint darker green leaves in various spaces, balancing the distribution. Choose a lighter green, and fill in the crown, making sure that there is a harmonious pattern.

2 Paint circle to represent oranges. Position them to suit your taste. Here the placement is random rather than balanced.

Techniques in context

Circles and crescents can contribute greatly to designs from nature. A variety of crescents is invaluable for creating realistic effects of movement and shading to convey a fresh, lifelike quality.

Clematis and Daisies

Judith Westegaard

Many techniques were used here, but the daisy petals are of particular interest. The basic strokes are mainly irregular commas, and the larger petals are overlaid with smaller ones. Note how many of the white strokes were shaded, using sideloaded crescent strokes – some regular, some ruffled. This technique is especially noticeable on the larger flower.

Scenic Recipe Clipping Desk

Prudy E. Vannier

Native scenes are increasingly popular subjects for decorative painters. The background of this picture was painted first in strips of color from top to bottom – using a flat brush. Then the demarcations of each area were established, utilizing the sideload method, before the detail was painted in.

1 Begin on the tip of the round brush, moving in a straight line.
2 Gradually apply pressure, flattening the hairs as the line lengthens.
3 When the hairs are flattened to the desired fullness, come to a full stop. Stand the brush up and lift off cleanly.

Grace Barnsley Arts and Crafts Design

Grace Barnsley was a ceramics painter for the famous British firm of Wedgwood and, like many designers, she used decorative painting techniques. This pretty Arts and Crafts design appears on a cream pitcher (jug) now on display in the Cheltenham City Museum, England. It features a "sit-down" teardrop stroke for the petals.

Teardrop

This is a versatile stroke because it can begin at the plump or the thin end. Starting from the thin end and finishing at the plump end is a "sit-down" teardrop; whereas painted from the other direction, it is best described as a "pull" teardrop (see pp. 80–81).

A "perfect" stroke is a flawless teardrop shape, and the paint has a smooth finish; an "imperfect" stroke, on the other hand, can be turned to advantage. For example, if you stand the brush up too quickly, the paint surface at the full end looks slightly crackly, but that can be an interesting effect in itself.

1 **Paint the large blue florals first. Outline the basic shape of each floral as a guide, so that the sit-down teardrop petals form a radiating flower head. Start with the central stroke and work outward in pairs on either side.**

Peacock

This colorful bird introduces one of the metallic paints: burnished copper. Some of the sit-down teardrops in the plumes have comma shapes yet are produced by the sit-down method.

1 *Trace the outline of the pattern on p. 121. Basing in with white flowing strokes gives overlaying colors vibrancy. Add extender (see p. 14) to the paint for smoother coverage. Allow to dry.*

2 *With extender blended into a round brush, pick up a small amount of bright blue to base the body. Before the paint dries, clean your brush and blot out the excess water. Now use this damp brush to lift off the blue paint with comma and S strokes (see pp. 54–55 and 66–67), to expose the white base underneath.*

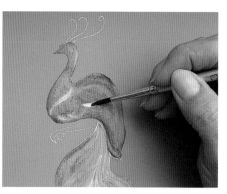

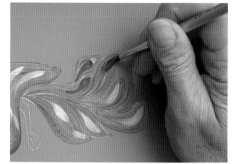

3 *Base the plumes with a contrasting blue shade mixed with extender. Remove paint in the center of each plume with a clean damp brush as in Step 2. Add shade to the breast, back and head. Paint bright blue sit-down teardrops over the areas where paint was removed. Again, remove the paint from the center of each of these strokes, using a smaller damp brush. Now fill these spaces with bright-green sit-downs (see picture for Step 4.)*

2 The last pair of sit-down teardrops is painted like this, completing the outlined space illustrated in Step 1.

3 Add the bunches of dots. Work from the bottom to the top of each bunch in rows. Use a stylus instead of a brush tip for this job.

4 With a liner brush, paint the branches and the tendril curlicues. The brush action for these is a movement from the shoulder, instead of the wrist and fingers. This movement is one you will need to practice, but you will notice that it gives you more control over the flow of the curly stroke and the paint.

4 *Outline the eye of each plume with orange. Then lightly outline each main plume with a dark-tone blue.*

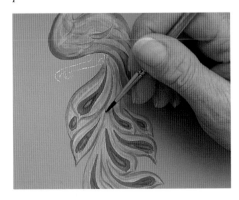

5 *Add green sit-down teardrops to the body over areas showing white base. Then, paint the comb, beak, legs and feet. Finally paint in the burnished copper plumes, as illustrated, and the comma and S flecks on the body.*

1 Press a fully loaded round brush onto the surface.

2 Pull the stroke toward you, gradually releasing pressure.

3 Allow the stroke to tail off and lift cleanly.

Pull Teardrop

Pull teardrops begin at the plump end before tailing off. These strokes can be painted to appear swollen with short tails, as shown in the wheat example, or in the sleeker form seen in the lace pattern variation.

Wheat

Many floral, fruit and plant images lend themselves to the pull teardrop stroke, since it gives a clean, natural look to some types of petals, seeds or the heads of wheat, as you can see in this example. This pleasing design can be used by itself on a breadbox or flour jar – or as part of a rural scene on a kitchen shade (blind).

1 Trace on the wheat pattern from p. 121 in chalk pencil. Begin painting at the top of each head of wheat. Each kernel is a pull teardrop, using a round brush loaded with a light-tone paint tipped with a darker tone, as shown.

VARIATION • 1

Lace

This is a sleek example of the pull teardrop. Extender (see p. 14) is mixed with white to give the lace a transparent, flimsy look.

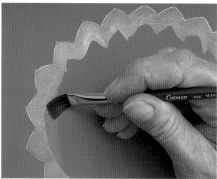

1 Trace the pattern on page 120. Using a flat brush, blend extender with a little white paint and underpaint the lace border (see Step 2). Do not worry about going over the inside line.

2 Clean the brush and blot out the excess water. Now take it around the inside edge of the lace border, cleaning off the paint that went over the line as you were underpainting.

Underpainting is a term used when a section of a design is painted with the intention of painting more detail over it.

3 Allow this transparent coat to dry. You can tell it is dry when the paint loses its sheen. Add the border, using the graduated dot stroke (see pp. 52–53).

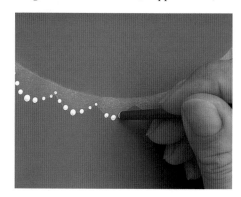

2 The kernels are painted from top to bottom, each kernel slotted beneath the other with a slight overlap as they progress down the head of wheat.

3 Using a liner brush, paint the stalks in a dark-toned green up to the base of each head of wheat.

4 Add the leaves, using a round brush loaded with a light-toned green for some parts of the leaves and dark-toned for others, as shown, to give the effect of the leaf color variations found in nature.

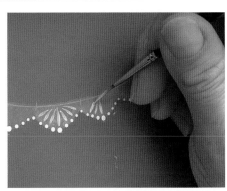

5 Paint the motif in the center of the pattern using pull teardrops. It will be more comfortable if you move the piece around as you work to find the most comfortable painting angle. Decorate around the border with the motif featured here or one of your own choice.

4 *Wait for the dots to dry before you proceed, because they are easily smudged. Add the pull teardrops from the outer edge in – remember this is a sleek stroke with long, clean tails to finish. Work from the middle of each scallop, radiating in a fan-like design as shown in the picture.*

1 Press down on a fully loaded round brush.

2 Pull it toward you, making a full stroke, and then begin to release pressure.

3 As you release pressure, start to squiggle, then tail off.

Squiggly Stroke

This stroke is painted with a round or liner brush. It can be a teardrop squiggly or a comma squiggly. Whichever shape, the tail wobbles. It can be a controlled or an irregular wobble. Another variety of this stroke has the squiggle emerging from the plump end. The fanciful floral below illustrates this.

Rosebuds

The squiggly stroke has many uses, either in a main image or as a finishing touch. Here the sepals illustrate the squiggle.

The rosebuds use the double loading method (see pp. 110–111).

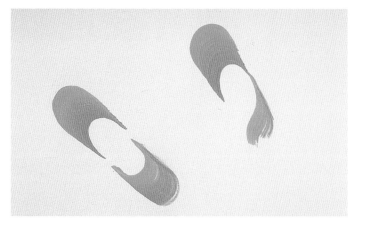

1 **To paint the rosebuds, use a flat brush, double loaded with a light and dark tone. For the rosebud on the left, paint two arched crescents (see p. 72). For the right-hand flower, finish an arched crescent with an S stroke, as shown.**

VARIATION • 1

Fanciful Floral

This example features the reverse squiggly teardrop with the squiggle emerging from the plump rather than the thin end.

1 Outline a faint ellipse in chalk. Paint four squiggly teardrops at 12, 3, 6 and 9 o'clock positions, then fill in the gaps with two more strokes.

2 Add dark squiggles between each turquoise stroke. These darker strokes should be shorter than the others – the circle guideline will help here.

3 Dot yellow paint at the center with the wooden handle of your brush. Paint the stem with a liner. The leaves are painted as squiggly strokes.

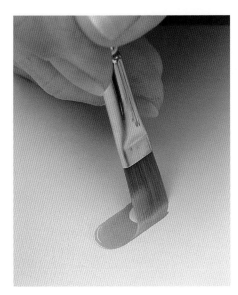

2 Paint a dipped crescent onto the rosebud on the left, overlapping the arched crescent just enough to close the gap between the two petals.

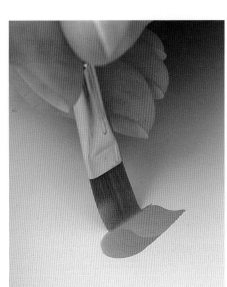

3 On the second rosebud, paint an S stroke to fill the unpainted area.

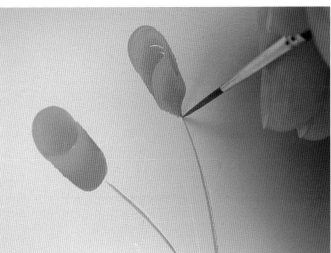

4 Paint the stems using a fine liner brush. Remember to bring the stems up to the base of each flower.

VARIATION • 2

Grain

Here the squiggles emerge from a very plump stroke. The brush is loaded with yellow, tipped with burnt sienna.

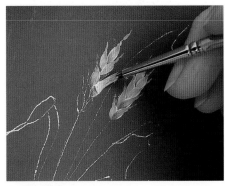

1 *Trace the pattern on p. 121. Begin each squiggly stroke at the top of the head of grain, working down from left to right, overlapping slightly.*

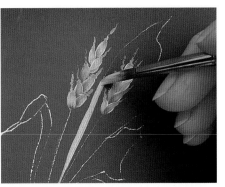

2 *Paint the stems with a liner brush and add the leaves with a round brush loaded with yellow.*

3 *The leaves adopt no stroke format. Follow the tracing lines, building the stroke in the direction of growth, and tail off with a slight squiggle.*

5 Paint the sepals, using a squiggly teardrop stroke. Paint the two outer ones first, and place the third off-center.

6 Irregular S stroke leaves were added, and the extra sepals of the second rosebud are fine lines emerging from behind.

VARIATION • 3

Vegetables

Vegetables provide diverse material for the use of squiggly strokes.

1 *Trace the vegetables from p. 120. The carrots, green onion (spring onion) roots and tomato sepals are all painted using squiggly teardrops.*

2 *Paint the onion with a brush loaded with a green tone tipped in white; the tomato is based in (see pp. 96–97); the carrot tips are squiggly strokes.*

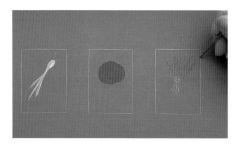

3 *The details were added mainly using squiggly strokes, such as the leaves of the carrots.*

Techniques in context

It is helpful to study traditional styles of decorative painting and to identify the strokes used, which can be relatively easy. In these examples, standard and sit-down teardrops are charmingly combined with other familiar strokes: the dot, comma and S stroke.

Bavarian-style Plates

Ann Wilson

These examples belong to the Bavarian school of decorative painting known as Bauernmalerei. The strokes were painted with a round brush, using simple teardrop, comma and S strokes. Loading two or three colors, undermixed in the brush (see p. 47), and painting wet-on-wet are also features of this style.

Bird Wall Plate

Lana Williams

Traditional designs using a limited stroke repertoire are a good choice for beginners. The daisies consist of sit-down teardrops; the stylized rose border, comma strokes. The choice of earth colors, along with dot accents and mini motifs, make this an especially attractive piece.

1 Begin on the tip, gently applying more pressure as you slide into a curve.

2 Just as you feel comfortable and in your stride, change direction abruptly.

3 Flip the brush into a hook stroke as shown.

Hooked Stroke

Painters in the East delighted in inventive strokework, some examples looked more complicated than they were. As you go through this book you may find that strokes such as the hooked stroke look difficult but are quite simple once you have practiced them. You will amaze yourself with your own dexterity!

For this stroke you should use a round or liner brush. Springy bristles help when producing the hook, which is a bit like doing a back-flip with the brush.

Foxgloves

Many flowering plants, such as the foxglove and snapdragon, lend themselves to the hooked stroke. This motif could be used as a large central image on an object, such as a tray, or in a montage of garden plant wall-decorations to brighten a room with images from nature.

1 **Some of the flowers will overlap the leaves, so you should start by painting the leaves. Using a round brush, paint comma or scroll strokes, moving from the plump part of the leaf toward the thin end, where the leaf joins the stalk.**

Owl in flight

Only a few of the strokes in this design are hooked, but their inclusion enhances the overall effect.

1 *Trace on the pattern from p. 122. Then, paint the moon with a circle stroke (see p. 74). Re-trace the design details over the moon.*

2 *Using a round brush, paint brown comma strokes on either side of the body. Then add the tail feathers using teardrop strokes.*

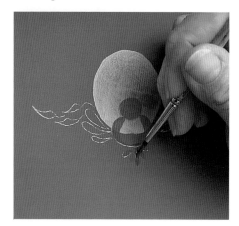

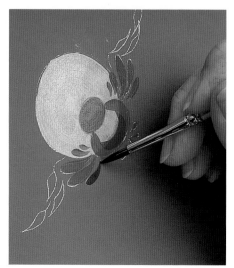

3 *The stylized outstretched wings use comma strokes in brown for the segments closest to the body.*

② Once you have painted the darker-toned stalks you can start the flowers, using the hooked stroke. Begin with the small ones at the top.

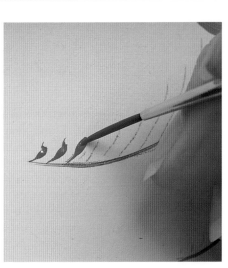

③ Gradually make the strokes longer and thicker as you move down the stalk. The hook at the tip of each flower should be kept small. Aim for a pleasing curve to the outside line of the flowers which mirrors the curve of the stalk.

⑤ You can finish off the tips of the flowers with the help of a stylus.

④ Finish the leaves by adding an off-center vein with a liner brush in the darker-tone green used for the stalks. You are aiming for a natural curve to give the impression of the main fold of the leaf.

---

4 *Base in the crescent of the body (see pp. 96–97), using dark brown. Add two flat comma strokes for the ears. Finish the wings by painting hooked strokes on the outer segments. The hooks should point upward to give the impression of flight.*

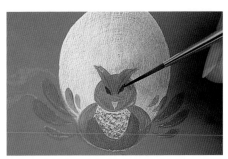

5 *The body feathers are made with dabs of a dry brushing (see pp. 44–45.) The eyes are painted using a liner brush in dark brown or black.*

6 *This is an excellent theme for a bedroom window shade (blind). Decorative paints can be used on fabric with the addition of fabric medium (see p. 14).*

1 Press your brush down flat onto the surface.

2 Raise the brush so that the tip is at the center of the "dollop."

3 Pull out of the dollop from the center, or from any point you choose, with the tip of your brush.

Dollop Strokes

The basic procedure for these strokes is to press a dollop of paint onto the surface. Then, by standing the tip of the brush up in the middle of the dollop and dragging it out a short distance from the top, you get a shape a bit like a dollop of meringue or a chocolate chip. Variations can be made by standing and dragging from different points of the dollop, as shown in the loon example, below.

Forget-Me-Nots

This forget-me-not garland is complemented by dainty sprigs of drooping greenery painted with the dollop stroke.

1 **The forget-me-not petals are created using eraser dot strokes (see p. 53). Position the flowers in a haphazard garland formation. Add highlighting dots in yellow to a few of the flowers. Next add the green stems with a liner.**

2 **Now add dollop strokes to imitate delicate leaves, which diminish in size as you go down the stems.**

(see p. 53)

VARIATION • I

Loon

Simple silhouettes of swimming birds are easy using the dollop stroke. Here, the stroke was adapted to depict long-necked loons, but ducks, geese and even swans are charming variations.

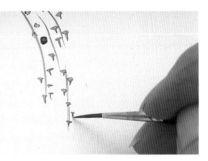

2 Paint another smaller dollop for the head, dragging out the beak in a horizontal direction.

3 Loons have white markings and these are added using dot strokes with a fine brush. If you are depicting another type of bird, choose the most striking element of its marking and paint it using very simple, fine strokes.

1 Drag out the loon's neck in a vertical direction from the side of the dollop.

Paddle Stroke

The paddle stroke is a teardrop with "shoulders." Instead of progressing smoothly from the tip to laying down the hairs of the brush gently, you sit down promptly when the tip reaches the required length. The stroke can be straight or curved.

1 With a round brush, glide down onto the tip.
2 Sit the brush down abruptly when the tip length is satisfactory.
3 Lift the brush off cleanly.

Cornflower

This attractive flower design, wth plenty of petals packed together, is great fun to paint using the paddle stroke.

1 Paint a yellow flower center. Begin your strokes on the yellow disk, painting around a circle. You will find it easier to turn your work instead of moving your hand.

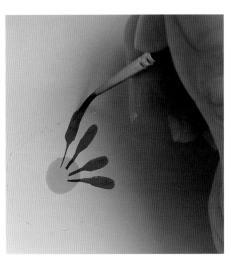

2 Paint another layer of paddle strokes over the first, which should have dried slightly. You can experiment with more or fewer petals strokes. Add a stem and paddle stroke leaves to finish.

VARIATION • I

Floral Sprig

Sprig arrangements are useful as fillers in an overall design. The leaves of this example are made with paddle strokes.

2 *Paint in the flower stems with a liner. Then paint a few paddle stroke leaves, varying in size, coming from the point where the stems meet.*

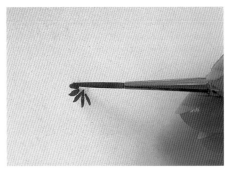

I *Paint some daisy style florals, using comma stroke petals arranged around yellow centers.*

3 *You see similar, simple flowering plant motifs in European medieval paintings, which inspired many of the great decorative artists of the 19th century.*

1 Flatten the hairs of a round brush until the tip is feathery.

2 Pick up a small amount of paint, and blend it into the brush on a palette.

3 Lightly pat the surface, depositing a suggestion of tracks.

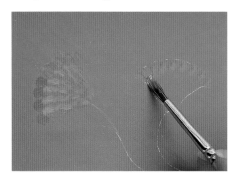

Pat Stroke

Pat strokes can be painted with any brush depending on the shape of the pat required. A round brush produces a curved pat; a flat brush can create either a square or chisel pat. Remember to blend the paint into the hairs of the brush on the palette before you make your strokes to ensure that the consistency is very light. This is a delicate stroke, so it does not need a lot of paint.

Spearhead

Floral patterns often benefit from the addition of soft accents as a contrast to sturdy stems and leaves. Pat strokes are ideal for giving a light, feathery effect to your floral designs.

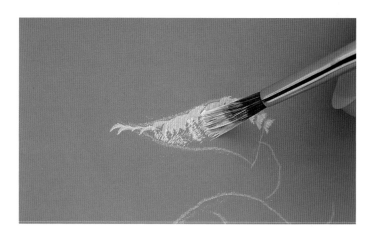

1 Trace on the pattern from page 122. Using a flattened round brush, paint pat strokes to create the spearhead flowers, beginning at the tip and working toward the base of the blossom.

VARIATION • I

Mophead

Here, the flattened brush hairs are double-loaded with small amounts of red and yellow, taking care not to overmix.

2 Paint the sepals with green squiggly teardrop strokes (see pp. 82–84) in a concentric pattern radiating from the center of the flower's base.

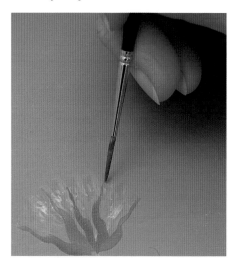

1 Trace the outline of the design, (see p. 123), in chalk. Using curved pat strokes, paint along the wide top of the flower, working down to the base, overlapping the previous rows of strokes.

3 Add the stems using a liner brush and finish with the leaves, which are ended with squiggly teardrop strokes.

2 Pat some strong highlights along one side of the spearheads.

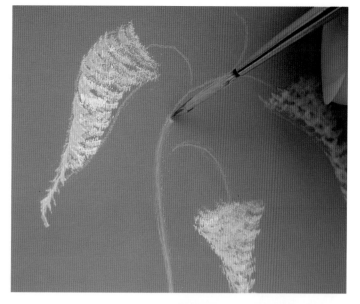

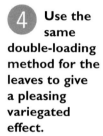

3 Double load a liner brush with two suitable stem colors (see pp. 110–111). Do not overblend the paints. Paint the stems in a long flowing stroke from bottom to top, ending at the center of the base of each flower.

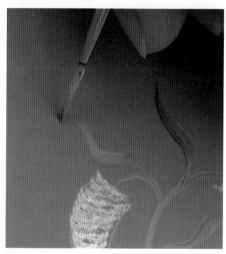

4 Use the same double-loading method for the leaves to give a pleasing variegated effect.

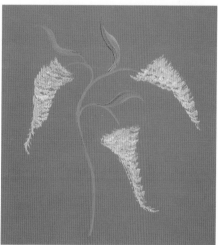

5 Try painting this motif with a variety of colors, such as two-tone blue flowers with green or deep purple stems and leaves.

VARIATION • 2

Cat

One of the main uses of pat stroke is for fur or scale details on animal designs.

2 *Pat on some fur highlights, using curved pat strokes with a flattened round brush. The highlights also give the illusion of a rounded body.*

1 *Trace the pattern outline, from page 123, in chalk. Base in the cat shape with black paint (see "basing", pp. 96–97). Retrace the detail over the top and paint on the outline details.*

3 *Paint the eyes, with a round brush and add white highlights to the edges of the pupils. Or, you can paint the eyes as eraser dot strokes (see p. 53), as shown in this picture.*

Techniques in context

The advantages of pat strokes for softening outlines and giving a convincing portrayal of features such as hair and fur are well illustrated here – from animal subjects to soft toys and an angel's curls.

Christmas Angel Plate

Lana Williams

Pat strokes were used for the lower part of the angel's hair to give a tightly curled look. The strokes were applied over a darker background, which creates the shadows among the curls.

Great Expectations

Judith Westegaard

This charming picture was created by drybrushing combined with pat strokes, an effective method for indefinite images, and for softening lines that need to remain imprecise.

It's for the Birds

Judith Westegaard

An accomplished artist combines a variety of techniques, responding spontaneously to the way the paint behaves: a pat stroke here, a finger dab there, and an overlay of drybrushing to soften line work. Adding extender to the pigment allows more time for such detailed work.

Baby's First Horsey

Kathye Begala

A charming nursery motif featuring traditionally favorite toys, including the rocking horse on which it is painted. The teddy bear and dog are achieved with pat blending, a technique often used to create a fuzzy or woolly effect.

Bold Painting

Bold painting, best described as a form of coloring-book painting, is the starting point for many people who begin this hobby. It uses four main techniques: color blocking or basing, color washing, line, and simple sideloading. These techniques considerably widen your scope. Bold painting frees you from the constraints of strokework and enables you to depict a more varied range of images, although you can, of course, incorporate strokes into a design – and many projects benefit from them. It is purely a matter of what suits you best as a technique or a design.

One of the most appealing aspects of bold painting is the use of sideloading, which makes your images stand out dramatically. This can be a revelation, giving you a real feeling of accomplishment.

These uncomplicated techniques can provide tremendous enjoyment. Very quickly and without too much practice, you can transform and decorate everyday objects.

1 Apply the first coat with a fully loaded brush. Allow to dry.

2 The second coat is applied in the same way and allowed to dry.

3 A third coat is applied to ensure thorough coverage.

Color Blocking

Blocking in color, also called "basing" or to "base in," creates an opaque surface coat onto which other design elements are painted. This is the starting point for most decorative painting images. Haphazard basing will not ruin your project, but a good job will show – lifting the quality of your work to a new plane. It is, of course, also possible to create a haphazard base for deliberate effect, but that is a matter of personal style.

For a smooth finish, apply the paint with a fully loaded brush, base coat upon base coat, until the appearance is even. Three coats is usual for most pigments, perhaps more if you are covering a dark background with a light pigment. Allow the paint to dry between applications. Use a hairdryer to speed things up.

Santa Claus

This design would be perfect for a Christmas wall plaque for you to keep and use year after year.
If you have never painted before, this is an easy and satisfying project. Paint the snowscape first, using basic background techniques described on pp. 34–37.

1 Paint the snowscape and apply the trace pattern, from p. 123. Base in the main elements, such as the hat, suit, face, boots, tree and belt. Three coats for each should be fine.

VARIATION • 1

Angel

The Angel's garment is blocked in and then given definition by using the sideloading method.

1 *The wings are painted as a wash (see pp. 100–101). Thin the pigment with extender, (see p. 14) rather than water to ensure an even application. Allow this layer to dry thoroughly.*

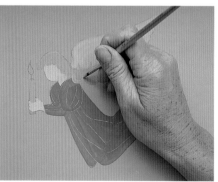

2 *Base in the hair and dress, each with a fully loaded brush. For the hair, tip a thin brush with a contrasting tone and suggest the curls with comma and long comma strokes.*

3 *The garment folds are shaded with a sideloaded flat brush. Use you own judgment to ensure a flowing effect to the fabric.*

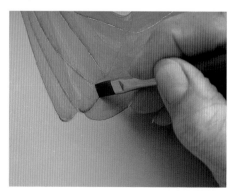

2 Paint haphazardly to create the furry effect of the hat trim with a round brush. Use teardrop and comma strokes for the beard. Add the mustache that you can see in Step 4.

3 Paint the tree ornaments and trunk, and finish the tree by drawing black outlines around the edges of the foliage (see final picture).

4 Retrace the facial features and paint the eyes, nose and cheeks. Finish Santa's outfit by adding the belt buckle and mittens. Outline all the details and apply shading, using a simple sideloading method (see pp. 102–103).

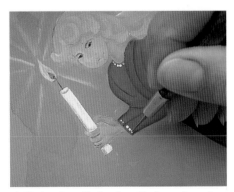

4 *Paint in all the detail: face, hands, feet and candle. The flare of the candlelight is created with sideloaded strokes. Use a stylus to suggest the trim of the garment, around the neck, cuff and tabard hem (refer to final picture).*

5 *Sideload a flat brush with silver pigment and paint the wing segments, as shown.*

| 1 Outlining with a liner brush. |
| 2 Outlining with a permanent ink pen. |
| 3 Outlining with a permanent brush pen. |

Line Work

Line work is mainly used to outline images and their detail, and is usually applied when a project is nearly complete. Fancy line work, such as scrolls, corkscrews and hatching are used as decorative embellishments and in some cases become the major feature of a design.

Line work can be done with a brush, a permanent brush pen or a permanent ink pen. Most beginners choose a disposable permanent pen. It is easier to control than a brush, the ink runs smoothly over acrylic paint, and it can be used against a ruler to create straight edges. The main advantage, however, is the permanence of the ink. Once dry, it will not come off or run. Before it dries, you have a small margin of time to correct mistakes by removing them with a damp brush.

Home Sweet Home

This project is painstaking due to the small scale, but it is not difficult. The final touches and the lines really bring the pattern to life.

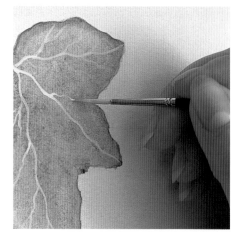

1 Base in the main elements of the design with three coats, or more if necessary. Some pigments cover better than others.

VARIATION • I

Ivy

The ivy design shows how line work can be used to delineate veins and tendrils – especially in styles of decorative painting other than bold painting.

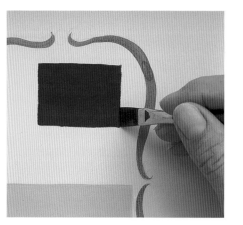

2 *Put in the main veins in white or light green using a liner brush, size No. 2 would be suitable.*

1 *Draw the outline of the ivy leaf and wet the leaf area slightly. Now wash a variety of colors, such as ultramarine, ochre yellow, and green (see pp.100–101) onto the surface using a soft brush.*

3 *Now paint the secondary veins using a finer brush, for example, size No. 1 if you used the size up for the main veins.*

2 Base in some of the objects. Plan the direction of your strokes to complement the shapes. For example, use flat comma strokes to base in the flag. Apply flat broad strokes for the book, and crescents for the apples.

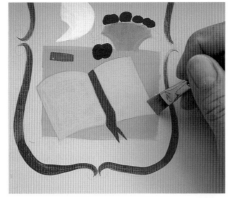

3 Add some of the details: the book cover, apple leaves, flag details and basket strokes.

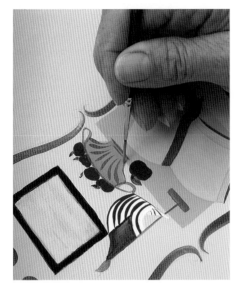

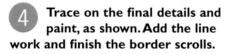

4 Trace on the final details and paint, as shown. Add the line work and finish the border scrolls.

4 *Add dark green shading along one side of all of the veins as shown. Use the same size brush as you used when painting the vein.*

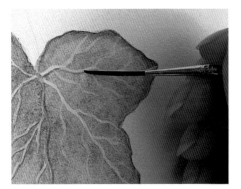

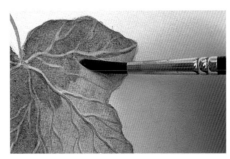

5 *Add a clear glaze medium (see p.14) to a mixture of green and ochre pigment and glaze the area of the leaf.*

6 *Paint in the stem and add tendrils in flowing long liner strokes to finish the design.*

I The background shows up brightly behind a single wash. Allow it to dry before second application.

2 The background is slightly less bright after the second wash but still visible.

3 With the third wash, the background becomes more subtle and light.

Dancing Partners

In this example, several washes were applied. The effect is more subtle than heavily applied coats with full loading.

Washing

Color washing produces a pleasing translucent effect. The pigment is diluted and applied as a thin watery coat. Several washes can be applied, but each must dry before a further application.

Dilute the paint with water or extender (see p.14) as much as necessary for the effect you want. The extender performs the same function as it does for basing in (see pp. 96–97). The convention in decorative painting is to aim for a uniform wash. To ensure evenness, prepare your wash to the desired dilution in a bubble palette. The tiny grains in acrylic pigments soon separate, so mix the solution repeatedly with your brush as you pick up more paint or add another coat. If you want a grainy wash effect, use a solution that is not homogeneously mixed.

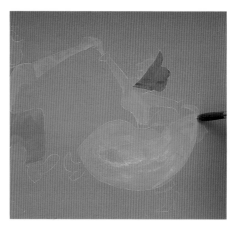

1 Apply the first wash to all areas except boots and sash. A round flattened brush is ideal for washing.

Swan

This example shows effective use of the wash technique in a subtler version than bold painting.

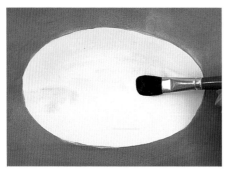

I *Outline the oval and wet the area. Add a graduating wash from top to bottom.*

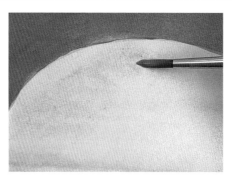

2 *While the background is still wet add a crimson wash in a line across the horizon. Add a green-toned wash to the water area. Then add a zigzag line of yellow wash in the top left area of the sky to produce an effect of hazy sunlight.*

3 *Paint a watery, wiggly line in a warm-toned red or brown along the horizon line to produce the effect of distant hills.*

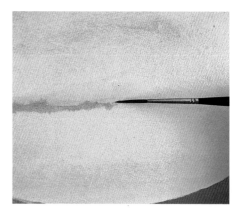

② **Apply a second wash over the same areas, following the various elements. Allow to dry.**

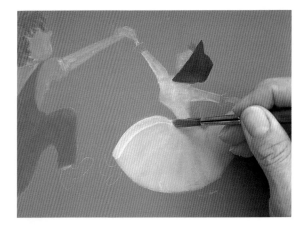

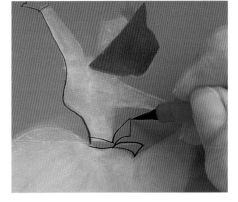

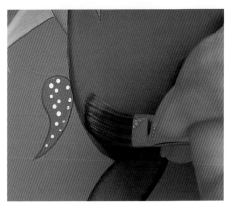

③ **Apply the third wash in the same way. Note how the background still glimmers through the washes.**

④ **Add all of the outlines. A brush pen is used here but practice with the other tools used for lining you have been shown in line work on the previous pages.**

⑤ **Add all of the detail, basing in the shoes, handkerchief, and so on. Shading on the overalls and suggesting the skirt gathers is done with a sideloaded brush.**

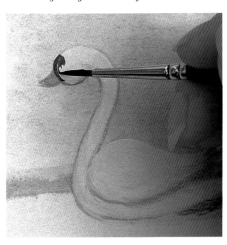

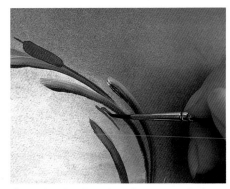

4 *Base in the swan in cream using a round brush. In a darker tone, such as raw umber, shade along the underside of the head, and outline the neck. Using light comma strokes, shade the underside of the wings and tail, as shown.*

5 *Highlight the swan in white and add the yellow beak and draw the details of the face and eyes in black.*

6 *Add a border of rushes around the oval to finish the design.*

1 Dilute paint with water or extender (see p. 14) to creamy consistency.

2 Dip one corner of a dampened flat or angled brush into the diluted paint.

3 A graduated color flows from the brush and enables you to create shades and highlights.

Urn with Birds

The charm of this design is its simplicity. The shaded two-tone effect provides a subtle but striking contrast to the more solid blue and white theme.

Sideloading

This technique makes your images come to life. It works by shading the main contours and some details of the image. You can use a flat or angled brush – the angled brush makes the technique simpler. Put a small amount of your selected shading pigment into a bubble palette. Dilute the pigment to a creamy consistency with a little water or extender (see p. 14). The extender is useful if you are shading large areas. Wet your brush in water and blot out the excess on a paper towel. Dip the corner of the brush into the diluted pigment. Place the dipped side next to the area you want to shade, and begin running the brush alongside it. If the paint starts to run out, re-dip as above, and resume where you left off, overlapping slightly with the previous stroke. Go over the entire stroke again to merge the point where the strokes joined.

1 **Trace the pattern from page 122. Use liner brush to outline stems and small birds. For the remainder of the outlining, use a sideloaded flat brush.**

VARIATION • 1

Christmas Duck

The border uses line work (see pp. 98–99) and sideloading to striking effect.

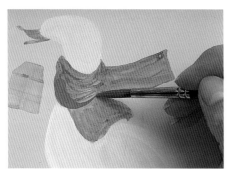

1 *Trace the pattern (see p. 124), and fill in the main elements, using the wash method (see pp. 100–101). The folds of the muffler (scarf) are shaded with a darker tone, using a round brush.*

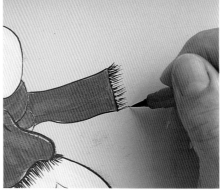

2 *A brush pen fitted with a cartridge is used here instead of an ordinary brush to outline the design and add fine detail. Unlike a brush, it can be used continuously, which is ideal for outline work.*

3 *Add some off-white wash onto the belly and the wing of the duck. Gray shading is applied to the underbelly, and feather outlines with a sideloaded flat brush.*

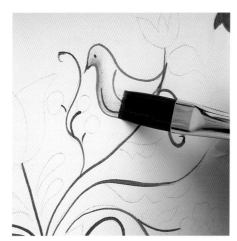

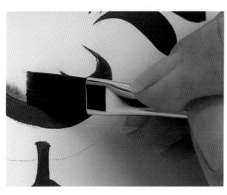

2 With a sideloaded brush, add the shading to the birds to create a suggestion of form. The eyes are dotted in with the wooden end of the brush.

3 Use a round brush to paint the comma stroke chicken plumes. Use the same brush to base in the wings, comb and feet.

4 With a sideloaded brush, outline the neck, neck ruffle and body outline (see final picture for reference). Add sideloaded shading to the wing outline you have just painted in **Step 3.**

5 Add white dots for the eyes with the wooden end of your brush to finish. This is a perfect design for showing the simplicity and charm of the simple sideloading technique.

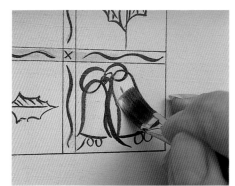

4 *A hint of yellow is sideloaded onto the bell to suggest its gold color.*

5 *One side of each of the holly leaves is highlighted with sideloading. Color is added to each of the flower blossoms, holly berries and the candy sticks, with sideloading strokes along the outlines. To add a speckled effect over the border, use an old toothbrush, lightly coated with burnt umber, to issue a fine spray of speckles as you gently draw your thumb back over the bristles. Take care not to speckle your duck too much!*

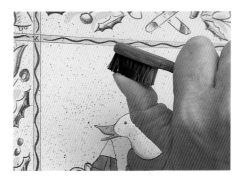

6 *Add sideloaded gray highlights to the outlines of the snowy ground. This picture could be used for a Christmas card for someone special, and can be framed and kept for a decoration.*

Techniques in context

The importance of good color blocking, or "basing in," is apparent in the quality of these examples, which also suggest where sideloading techniques or line work can be used most effectively.

Money Box, Pencil Box and Horses
Kate Mellor

Color blocking and line work are the main features of these pieces, and provide a particularly effective approach for children's images.

Birdhouse
Rhonda Thorne

A predominance of regular-shaped crescent strokes form each symmetrical petal, and sideloaded crescents outline the leaves. The drybrushed woodgrain effect is a fitting background for the birdhouse walls and roof.

Antique Tinware Tabletop
Nancy Bateman

Birds, florals, hearts and urns have been popular images through the ages. This example uses a stroke glazing technique to impart a transparent look, with the background shimmering through. The strokes are predominantly comma and S strokes. Sideloaded strokes are used to build up the body outlines of the birds. Complementary touches of glazing are added for subtle effect in just a few places.

Chef Pierre's Soup Pot

Prudy E. Vannier

Chef Pierre is painted, like the Santa Claus design on pp. 96–97, with the main area based in first. Shading and highlighting were achieved by lightly layering the paint with sideloaded flat brushes.

Blending Strokes

This section consolidates all of the skills learned so far and takes them to a more advanced level. Good blending depends on strokework, although the untrained eye might be unable to detect it. It also uses and extends the techniques covered in the preceding section. For example, the simple sideloading method (see pp. 49 and 102–103) is here developed to more sophisticated effect. We show you how to vary the width of the graduated line of color, and how to expand it into a series of strokes. These are the techniques that will enable you to make an object look photographically real, because they allow you to build up three-dimensional form.

How real you want your painting to look is a matter of personal taste. A slight impression or an approximation is perfectly acceptable. Avoid the overworked look.

1 With a dampened flat brush, pick up a small amount of paint on one corner.

2 Blend on the palette, going back and forth over a strip of approximately ½ in (13mm), so that the color graduates across the hairs.

3 The brush is now ready for painting using the sideloaded method.

Advanced Sideloading

This advanced sideloading technique can give your work a striking degree of reality, and the flexibility of artistic self-expression. Practice loading the brush. The trick is to gauge the right balance between the amount of water retained in the brush hairs and the amount of paint picked up on the corner of the brush. If you want a perfectly smooth look, the balance is delicate and the paint must be thoroughly blended on the palette. If you want a streaky effect, thorough blending is not crucial. Practice with different ratios of water to paint.

Two-tone Floral

In this project, the sideloaded strokes and streaks applied over an initial wash (see pp. 100–101) build to create an unusual floral pattern.

1 **Trace the pattern on p. 125. Add a light-green wash, using extender rather than water for the flowers and leaves. Move sympathetically with the shapes as you paint.**

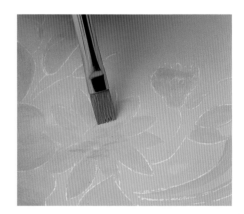

Lemon Tea

This still life uses sideloading to put highlighting and shading back to back, bringing the teapot into the 3-D plane.

1 *Trace the pattern from p. 125, and apply three base coats to the teapot and lemon. Retrace and paint the pattern. Shade the lemon by sideloading with a darker tone.*

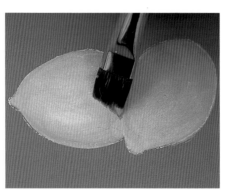

2 *Build up the lemon's form by adding more shades and highlights with the sideloaded brush.*

3 *Place the trace pattern over the teapot once more and trace the contour lines of the teapot. You can use a stylus or a pencil.*

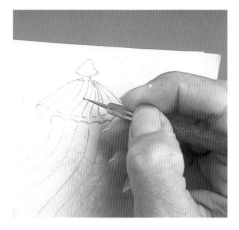

2 Use a darker shade of green wash to add tonal variation to the centers and bases of the florals. Begin adding white highlights with sideloaded strokes.

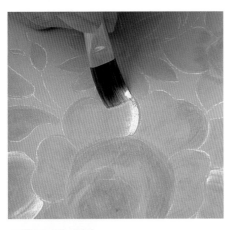

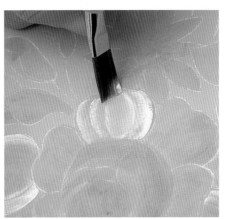

3 Applying several strokes as streaks to some of the petals makes the design interesting. Remember to flip your brush when you want to do right-sided curves.

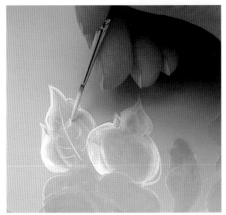

5 Finishing touches can be added by sideloading a flat brush and applying scrolls and flat commas in a darker tone to some of the white outlines of the foliage.

4 Sharpen the design in places by outlining the leaves and adding the veins in white with a liner brush.

6 The final result: sideloaded strokes and streaks, using white on a subdued background, create a soft classic look.

4 *Shade the crescent stroke on the base of the teapot and the top rim. Then follow the contour lines with a sideloaded angled brush, shading the right-hand side of each with gray and highlighting the left-hand side with white. The central highlights are longer strokes, diminishing as they move outward.*

5 *Sideload an angled brush with a darker shade tone, add shading to the spout opening, underside of spout and handle areas. Also shade underneath the lemons and the teapot.*

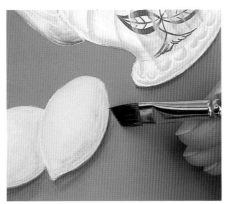

6 *The final result shows that the sideloading method enables you to achieve a good impression of realism.*

1 Dip each side of the flat brush into the individual paint puddles.
2 Blend on the palette to encourage the color to graduate and merge in the center.
3 The graduated, two-toned effect can be used in a range of ways.

Double Loading

This technique is very similar to sideloading. Use a dampened flat brush. Pick up different tones or colors of paint on each corner of the brush, then blend with the palette across a ¼–½in (6–12mm) strip until the colors gently graduate and merge.

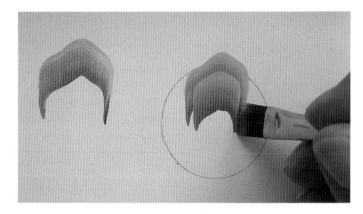

① You may find it easier to draw a circle outline as a guide to forming your rose, as shown on the right. It will help to show where each stroke is placed in relation to others. Using a double-loaded flat brush, paint two humped crescents, one overlapping the other and slightly smaller.

Classical Rose

Most painters aspire to portray the classical rose, and you may be amazed to discover that it consists of just a few double-loaded strokes. The trick is to put the strokes in exactly the right place. You will get the knack of this, so don't give up! It is advisable to reblend between each stroke, and to reload when necessary.

Some of the following stages overlap slightly in order to give you as much clear guidance as possible.

VARIATION • 1

Basket of eggs

The basket is constructed of a series of double-loaded S strokes. The brush has been loaded with a light and dark tone to maximize the basket work effect.

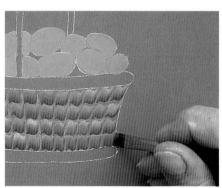

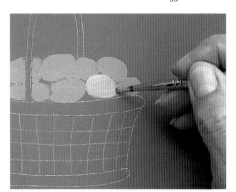

1 *Trace on a pattern and base in the eggs with three coats. Paint the eggs in the background first.*

2 *Now paint the wickerwork, using a double-loaded flat brush. Work in rows, moving left to right. Be consistent with each stroke, holding the brush so that the dark tones are toward the bottom of each stroke.*

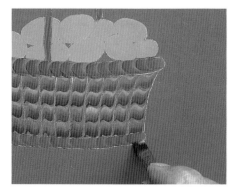

3 *Turn your brush and paint overlapping crescent strokes, as shown, at the top and bottom of the basket. Add the handle.*

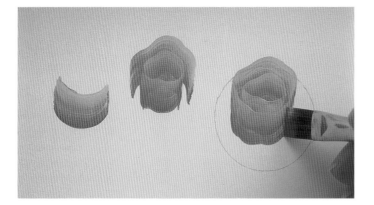

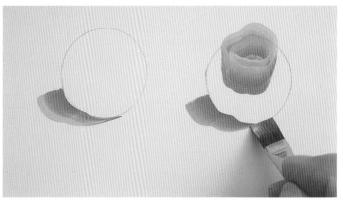

2 Now you will need to do the center and outer petals at the front. These crescents go in the opposite direction to the first pair. Again with a double-loaded flat brush, with the darker paint at the bottom, join the ends of the inside petal first. Introduce a small wobble in the crescent if necessary to close the gap in the center. Then join up the ends of the outer crescent.

3 The next stroke is a flat comma with a slight kink two-thirds into it. Think of the circle as a clockface. This comma starts at about 8 o'clock, and tails off between 5 and 6 o'clock. Placement can be as shown or it can be closer to the completed strokes.

4 Paint the same stroke from the opposite direction, scissoring the tails. Between this pair of strokes and the bowl of the rose, paint a regular pair of flat commas with scissored tails.

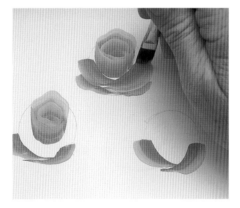

5 This is also a flat comma stroke, but note that it begins with the chisel tucked alongside the rose bowl and tails off at the bottom of the bowl.

4 Use the sideloading method (see pp. 102 and 108) to shade the eggs. Several applications might be needed. Allow each coat to dry before additional applications.

5 With a double-loaded brush, add the bow. Follow instructions for ribbons and bows on the next page.

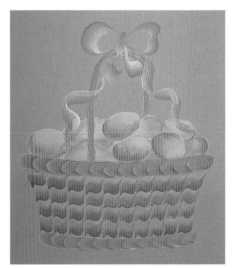

6 Bows can be all shapes and sizes. You will enjoy experimenting. You may wish to add some shading underneath the basket using the sideload method.

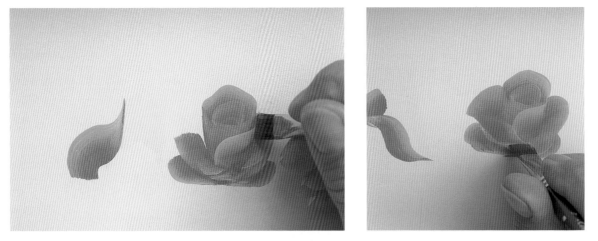

6 This is where it may all start to look confusing! Extend your powers of observation. This stroke begins where the last one ended, at the bottom of the bowl. Hold the brush horizontal to the bowl, swivel it around as though you are about to make a circle, but instead finish off as for an S stroke. The result is a rose missing a petal on the left-hand side. This is the final gap to be filled.

7 The finishing stroke is an acrobatic one, because the brush flips over two-thirds of the way down and goes into S stroke mode. The stroke begins along the left-hand side of the bowl, and its tail covers the horizontal part of the previous stroke.

8 To finish off the design, see p. 82–83 for rosebuds and p. 66 for the rope border.

To finish off the design, see p. 82–83 for rosebuds and p. 66 for the rope border.

VARIATION • 2

Ribbons and Bows

Ribbons and bows are combinations of crescent and S strokes made with a double-loaded flat brush. But instead of lifting the brush every time you complete a stroke, you run on into another stroke until your ribbon ends.

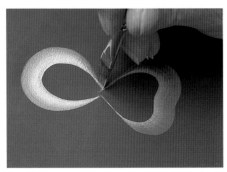

1 *Paint two crescents, one arched and one dipped, using well blended paint.*

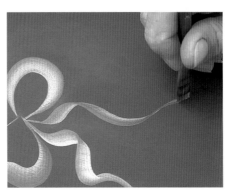

2 *To get the right effect of the ribbon ends curling you will need to practice this example many times. To reproduce the wavy line, hold the brush at right angles to the direction of the strokes. Then paint toward you.*

3 *Finish with a small crescent for the knot. As you can see from the "basket of eggs" design on the previous pages, bows can be used as part of another design or as a single motif.*

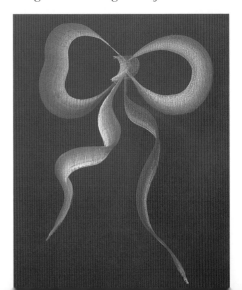

Techniques in context

Advanced sideloading and double-loading techniques open the way to a world of exquisite effects, both rich and delicate — epitomized by the multi-petaled rose but applicable to many still-life subjects.

Roses and Strawberries
Bette Byrd

Roses are a challenge to most painters. The more petals, the better! This artist loves an opportunity to show off her skills at overlaying double-loaded strokes to imitate the sublime delicacy of the old-fashioned rose.

Under the Mistletoe

Bobby Campbell

Beautifully blended candy canes and mistletoe are set against a dark background enhanced by the speckled effect. The speckling is very subtle but adds depth and interest to the piece.

Roses on apron

Bette Byrd

Here the artist has used sideloaded commas and crescents to make a pretty — yet durable — design for an apron. Decorative painting is wonderfully versatile, allowing the artist to use the same acrylic gouache paints on a variety of surfaces. Simply by adding a small amount of fabric medium (see p.14) to the pigment, you can paint on natural fabrics, such as cotton.

1 Basecoat with a rich, dark tone. Allow it to dry.

2 Apply a lighter toned wash (see pp. 100–101) over the basecoat. Allow to dry.

3 Apply the second wash in a medium tone. Note the subtle variations created through the layered effect.

Layering

Layering and blending techniques create translucence and depth which give your subject a realistic look. These techniques can be used together and you can go on refining the layers and blends – sometimes forever it seems. The trompe de l'oeil (deceptively likelike) effect is a good example. Impatient painters soon discover you can build up the layers quite quickly by painting wet-on-wet. The important thing is judging the amount of moisture in your brush and on your subject and getting the balance right. Dampening the brush with extender (see p. 14) rather than water may be helpful.

Apple

Here we demonstrate the application of a series of layered washes in various tones. A sublime quality of inner light is radiated. Layering is ideal for painting fruit; it gives a succulent sheen to the image which will make them irresistible.

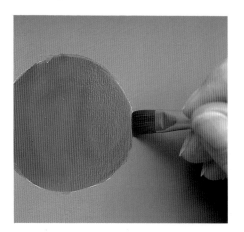

1 Apply the first wash. You might prefer to work with a flattened round brush, as shown in Step 3, instead of a flat brush. Many artists prefer it.

VARIATION • 1

Pear & Blackberries

Here, the pear is built up in layers. The blackberries rely more on a series of sideloaded crescent strokes (see pp. 70–71).

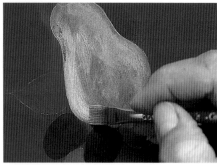

1 *Base in the pear, berries and leaves in their relevant colors. Leave to dry. Softly brush over a lighter tone on the left-hand side, as shown.*

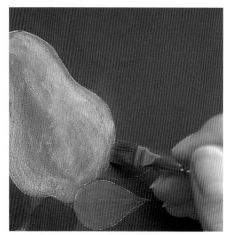

2 *Brush a even lighter toned wash over the right-hand side of the pear.*

3 *Base in the blackberry outlines, varying the tones of each, as shown. Then add a wash of green highlight onto the pear, using a sideloaded flat brush. Do not overblend on the palette, because a less blended stroke is more interesting.*

2 Once the first wash is dry use a brighter tone for the second wash. You can concentrate the wash on one side of the apple if you wish. Allow to dry.

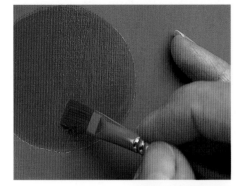

3 Now load your brush with a darker tone and blend it with flowing strokes into the apple image, following its contours. Note the slight streaky appearance. Allow to dry.

4 Blend some ashen tone highlights over the top, leaving some areas bare. This helps to diminish color uniformity and so create a more realistic look.

5 Now we bury all the washes, using a bright-toned wash. Barely visible under its surface, a multi-toned radiant translucence is emitted. Add the stem.

6 Finish by adding some highlights to indicate the direction of a light source, using dry-brushing strokes (see pp. 44–45).

4 *Fill in the blackberry outlines with crescent segment, using a sideloaded brush. Add a wash of a small amount of red into the plump part of the pear, use the final picture as a guide.*

5 *With liner, add a few strong highlights to each of the center and right-hand blackberries. Add the darker-toned green veins to the background leaves.*

6 *Add the stalks and leaves of the blackberries, using comma and squiggly teardrop stroke (see pp. 82–83). The stem of the pear has been painted in to complete the design.*

Techniques in context

Layering and blending techniques, along with the clever use of color, can create remarkable *trompe l'oeil* (lifelike) effects, delighting the eye and tricking it into perceiving depth and distance.

Christmas Memory Box

Trudy Beard

The snowy tonal vignette, created by subtle blending, is in dramatic contrast to the surrounding poinsettia motif, which utilizes an array of layering and blending techniques. A Christmas wreath and Cardinals link the framework to the landscape.

Vining Strawberries on Clam Steamer

Betty Herron

The popular choice for decorative painting is acrylic gouache. However, some artists prefer to work in oils, as in this example. The texture and longer drying time of oils makes them ideal for highly blended treatments. Here, colors and values were applied side by side, then blended lightly. As each layer dried, values were deepened or lightened by glazing.

Coffee Filter Box

Dorothy Whisenhunt

The bowl of fruit is a classic of decorative art, designed to show the painter's skill at blending. Here, each apple and pear is a perfect specimen, with the color built up in layers to convey an impression of inner light and juiciness. The grapes also are individually blended. Sideloaded strokes are integrated to create shades and highlights.

Harvest Box

Trudy Beard

The central vignette background was brushed on lightly, almost as a wash. Note how the line between land and sky is observed with a drybrushed blending technique. The frame of pumpkins and leaves was painted using a combination of blending methods, its rich colors lending distance to the scene.

Lettering and Numbers

From time to time, the need arises to incorporate lettering and/or numbering with a design. If you are painting a piece as a gift, the personalized touch of the recipient's name and the date brings great pleasure. A saying or a verse can also be a nice touch.

There are many styles of lettering and numerals, some easier to reproduce than others. Here, two models are provided. The uncial letters and numbers are made with a narrow flat brush, and the italic capitals with a scroller.

1 2 3 4 5 6 7 8 9

1 2 3 4 5 6 7 8 9 0

These numbers are in uncial (top) and italic, so that you can match them to the lettering you choose.

A B C D E
F G H I K L
M N O P Q Q
R S T U V V
X Y Z Z

This alphabet is in Roman capitals from a script dating back to the 2nd century AD. The letters "J" and "W" are not part of the script.

This is an example of uncial script.

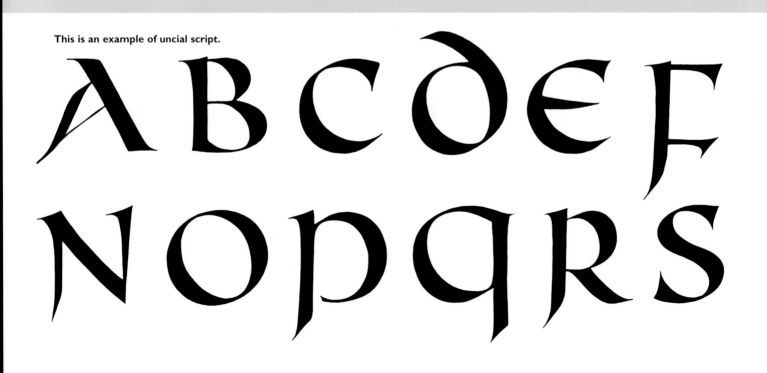

This alphabet is an italic script in upper and lower case.

Aa Bb Cc Dd Ee Ff
Gg Hh Ii Jj Kk Ll
Mm Nn Oo Pp Qq
Rr Ss Tt Uu Vv
Ww Xx Yy Zz

CHIJKLM
TUVWXYZ

Patterns

The following designs appear in this book and may be used for non-commercial purposes. They can be enlarged or reduced to suit your requirements.

Lace pp. 80–81

Vegetables p. 84

Peacock pp. 78–79

Guitar p. 67

Bluebell Sprigs p. 66

Wheat pp. 80–81

Grain p. 83

Tulip p. 55

Owl in Flight pp. 86–87

Urn with Birds pp. 102–103

Spearhead pp. 90–91

Mophead p. 90

Cat p. 91

Santa Claus pp. 96–97

Christmas Duck pp. 102–103

Two-tone Floral pp. 108–109

Lemon Tea pp. 108–109

Index

Page numbers in *italics* refer to illustrations

Credits

Quarto would like to thank all the artists who have kindly allowed us to reproduce their work in this book.

They can be contacted through Quarto.

Additional credits: page 2, above, by Judith Westegaard; page 3 by Trudy Beard; page 4 by Prudy E. Vannier; page 14, watering can by Priscilla Hauser, antique steamer by Nancy Bateman; page 15, apron by Bette Byrd; page 39, cabbage kitchen store cupboard by Prudy E. Vannier; page 45 grandmother clock by Ann Mary Lee; page 47, box painted by Lana Williams; page 59 photo courtesy of Elizabeth Whiting Associates; page 68, above left, by Kate Mellor, below by Rhonda Thorne; page 69, above, and page 70, by Onya Tolmasoff; page 104, below, photo by Greg Schultz.

All other photographs are the copyright of Quarto Publishing.

We would like to acknowledge and thank the following for supplying materials used in this book:

Blanks:
Scumble Goosie
Lewiston Mill
Brimscombe
Stroud
Gloucestershire
Great Britain
Tel: (01453) 731305

Pressed paper boards:
John Purcell Paper
15 Rumsey Road
London
SW9 OTR
Great Britain
Tel: (0171) 737 5199
Fax: (0171) 737 6765

Paints:
UK supplier of Jo Sonja products:
Tomas Seth and Company
Holly House
Castle Hill
Hartley
Kent
DA3 7BH
Great Britain
Tel: (01474) 705077
Fax: (01474) 703093

US supplier of Jo Sonja products:
Chroma Acrylics, Inc.
Bucky Drive
Lititz, PA 17543
USA
Tel: (800) 257 8278

UK supplier of Delta Ceramcoat products:
George Weil & Son Ltd
The Warehouse
Reading Circle Road
Redhill
Surrey, RH1 1HG
Great Britain

Delta Technical Coatings, Inc.
2550 Pellissier Place
Whittier
California, 90601-1505
USA
Tel: (800) 423-4135 or (213) 686-0678
Fax: (310) 695-5157

Brushes:
Loew Cornell Brushes
563 Chestnut Avenue
Teaneck
NJ 07666-2490
USA
Tel: (201) 836 7070
Fax: (201) 836 8110

Additional thanks to Prue Lester for providing illustration for pp. 16–19 (top), 64–65 (top), 98–99 and 100–101 (bottom).